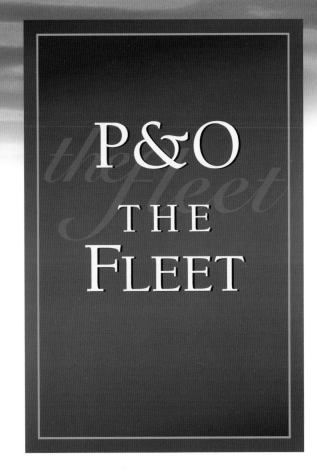

P&O THE FLEET

P&O the

Miles Cowsill · Joh.

Published by

FERRY *Publications*

ISBN 1-871947-54-5
Ferry Publications Ltd
PO Box 9, Narberth, Pembrokeshire SA68 0YT
Tel: +44(0)1834 891460   Fax: +44(0)1834 891463

CONTENTS

CHAPTER 1

P&O - A Brief History

The origins of The Peninsular and Oriental Steam Navigation Company can be traced as far back as 1815, when Brodie McGhie Willcox opened his ship-broking office in the city of London and engaged as his assistant a young Shetlander by the name of Arthur Anderson. By 1823 the firm had become Willcox and Anderson, and the business had expanded to include the operation of small sailing vessels to Spain and Portugal, as agents for the owners. In the early 1830's the partners began to charter steamers, including, in June 1834 the *Royal Tar*, owned by a group of Dublin businessmen led by Captain Richard Bourne RN, and it was to Bourne that they turned again in March 1835 when beginning a regular service with his *William Fawcett,* soon adopting the trading name Peninsular Steam Navigation Company. The following year the company's first owned ship, the newly built *Iberia* entered service on the route to Spain and Portugal, now extended to include Gibraltar.

The partners had raised loans, chartered steamers for use as troopships and warships, and engaged in gun running for the Royal Houses in both the Spanish and Portuguese Civil Wars in the early 1830's, and as a result, were granted the right to fly both sets of Royal Colours. That house-flag, bearing the red and yellow of Spain and the blue and white of Portugal, is still proudly flown today by the ships of

The Hindostan, 2,000 tons, sailing from Southampton for Calcutta on her first voyage on 24th September 1842. (P&O)

the P&O.

In 1836 responsibility for the carriage of mail by sea was transferred from the Post Office to the Admiralty, to whom the Company successfully tendered in 1837 for a mail contract between Falmouth, Vigo, Oporto, Lisbon, Cadiz and Gibraltar. The traditionally accepted founding date of P&O is 1st September 1837 - the day that the first mail steamer, the *Don Juan*, departed from London, collecting the mails from Falmouth four days later. While on the homeward run, the ship was lost on rocks off Tarifa Lighthouse, at the southernmost tip of the Peninsula, but the reputation of the Company survived, as all of the passengers, crew, mails and cargo were saved.

Mail contracts continued to be an important source of revenue and in 1839 the Company was awarded the contract to carry the mails between Falmouth and Alexandria via Gibraltar and Malta. As neither ships nor capital were available, a merger was agreed with the Trans-Atlantic Steamship Company of Liverpool, bringing two ships, the 1,300 ton *Great Liverpool* and the 1,600 ton new-building *Oriental* into the fleet. New capital was raised by setting up a company limited by Royal Charter, and thus The Peninsular and Oriental Steam Navigation Company was formally established on 31st December 1840 with a capital of £1m. The following year the UK terminus was moved to

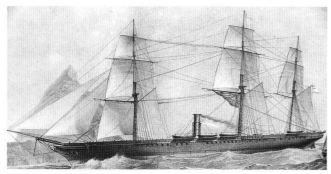

*The 3,400 ton **Himalaya** of 1854 served the company for only a few months before being sold to the British Government for use as a troopship. As a hulk, she survived until being bombed by German aircraft at Portland, Dorset in 1940. (P&O)*

Southampton, where it remained until 1881 before returning to London.

At the end of 1842 a Suez to Calcutta service was established, and a mail contract for the route was awarded from 1845. This necessitated transporting the mails and passengers overland from Alexandria, since the Suez Canal had yet to be built, to join a ship in Suez. This celebrated 'Overland Route' involved travel by canal boat from Alexandria to the Nile, then by river steamer to Cairo and finally by horse drawn coach to Suez. The mails, transported by camel, often arrived before the passengers.

Services to Singapore and Hong Kong began two years later and the extension of the mail contract to Sydney occurred in 1852. With its major routes now well established, the Iberian Peninsula service, on which the Company had been founded, was abandoned in 1862.

In 1844 the Company advertised a 'Grand Tour' by sea, sailing from Southampton to Gibraltar, Malta, Athens, Smyrna, Jaffa and Alexandria utilising three ships, the *Lady Mary Wood*, the *Tagus* and the *Iberia*. This voyage was recorded in William Makepeace Thackeray's 'Notes of a Journey from Cornhill to Grand Cairo'. While not a cruise in the modern sense, it is generally accepted that with this voyage P&O invented cruising. Subsequently a number of round voyages on one ship to destinations such as Constantinople and Alexandria were offered. Further development of these activities was curtailed by the outbreak of the Crimean War some ten years later.

P&O's involvement with trooping probably began in 1840 when the *Oriental* carried an artillery detachment to Malta. Subsequently, several of the Company's ships carried troops to outposts of the Empire to quell uprisings. The *Vectis*, on which Florence Nightingale travelled from Marseilles, was among the nine P&O ships involved in the Crimean War. Company ships were again in government service in the Persian Campaign of 1857, the Indian Mutiny of 1857/8, the Anglo French expedition to China in 1860 and the Abyssinian War of 1867/8.

Prior to 1851 the Company's vessels had been driven by paddle wheels. The *Shanghai*, delivered that year, was its first screw-driven ship, although sails would continue to be carried for extra speed and breakdown security for at least another four decades. It took the Admiralty some time to accept screw propulsion and to modify the mail contracts accordingly.

When the Suez Canal opened in 1869, most of the P&O fleet was rendered obsolete overnight. Ships had been built for the two different trades East and West of Suez, and the Company also had huge investments in infrastructure in Egypt. However, the British Authorities did not allow any amendment to the mail contract insisting that the mails still be unloaded at Alexandria and carried over-land to Suez. This condition was not removed until a new contract was negotiated in 1874. The Canal also radically changed the nature of the business of transportation by sea. Until then, generally the cargo carried by the Company east of Suez consisted of small high value items. With the opening of the Canal the carriage of lower value high volume goods by predominantly cargo carrying ships became an economic proposition. P&O decided to build new ships rather than modify the existing fleet, and seventeen entered service between 1871 and 1873, including a number with substantially increased cargo capacity.

Technical developments continued. The *Ravenna* of 1880 was the first ship to have a full steel superstructure, while the *Valetta* of 1884 became the first in the fleet to be fitted with electric light.

In 1887 to celebrate the Golden Jubilees of both Queen Victoria and the Company a new class of four large steamers was built. At 6,500 tons, the *Victoria*, *Britannia*, *Oceania* and *Arcadia* were the largest and most luxurious ships in the fleet. These were also among the first ships to have gun platforms incorporated into their design to allow easy conversion into armed merchant cruisers should the need arise which, in the case of these ships, never did.

*The 5,000 ton **Rome**, delivered in 1881, became the **Vectis** in 1904 and was then the Company's first permanent cruise ship.* (William Mayes collection)

In 1894 the *Britannia* and the *Victoria* were employed on long-term trooping contracts, and the Government quickly realised the advantages of chartering rather than owning their own vessels. Within six years P&O had taken delivery of its first purpose-built troopships, which were put on permanent charter to the British Government.

Spare capacity on ships between England and the Mediterranean (Government officials and those on business would often travel overland to Marseilles or Brindisi to save up to four days) was sold for short pleasure voyages, but it was not until 1904 that P&O advertised its first proper cruise to Norway aboard the 6,000 ton *Vectis*, which had been refitted to carry 150 first class passengers. Thus began the modern tradition of cruising with P&O. The *Vectis*, and later some of the larger M class ships continued this service until the outbreak of war in 1914. The M class of ten passenger liners was delivered between 1903 and 1911 and represented the largest building project to date for the Company. The early ships were 9,500 tons, but as the class progressed later ships were larger, with the final trio being 12,500 tons. The last ship of this class, the 1911-built *Medina*, was used as the Royal Yacht for King George V's tour to India later that year.

With the acquisition of Blue Anchor Line in 1910, a new third class only operation, known as the P&O Branch Service, began to Australia via the Cape. This represented a total digression from previous policy in that it gave P&O its first regular service via the Cape, and was also the Company's first venture into third class travel. This operation had to be kept separate from the main fleet activities by reason of Australian labour regulations and was a very successful venture, at least until the late 1920's. The five Blue Anchor ships taken over were quickly replaced with a series of new-buildings.

In October 1914 P&O took over the British India Steam Navigation Company, by means of an exchange of shares. British India operated an important network of routes east of Suez, which served as feeders for the P&O mail ships. The combined fleet at the time of the merger consisted of 197 ships (64 P&O, 133 British India). P&O and British India remained totally separate companies, but with a common board of directors, and as the BI Chairman, Lord Inchcape became Chairman of P&O. The deal could almost be described as a "reverse

The Narkunda, delivered by Harland & Wolff in 1920 for the Australian service, had been ordered by P&O in 1914. (William Mayes collection)

takeover", although the P&O Chairman Sir Thomas Sutherland took the credit at the time.

The other event of 1914 was to have even greater significance; the Company was relieved of almost two thirds of its fleet for war service. Ships were converted for use as armed merchant cruisers, troopships and hospital ships. During the course of the war P&O lost 17 ships, and several more were damaged in almost 100 attacks on the Company's ships.

P&O not only kept the supply and communication lifelines open with its much reduced fleet, but also expanded by means of acquisition of other companies. Amongst those to join the group during the war were New Zealand Shipping Company, Federal Steam

Navigation Company, William Cory & Son, Union Steamship Company of New Zealand, Hain Steamship Company and James Nourse. Together they lost 68 ships between being acquired by P&O and the end of hostilities. The most significant acquisition, as far as passenger services were concerned, came in December 1918, when a 51% stake was purchased in the Orient Steam Navigation Company, a joint operator with P&O on the Australian Mail Contract. Orient Line's origins could be traced back to the founding of London shipbrokers James Thompson & Company in 1797, although the Orient Line name did not come into usage until the sailing ship of that name was delivered in 1853. The Orient line had emerged from the war with a fleet of five mail steamers, having lost three ships to enemy action, and one, the *Otranto*, after a collision with P&O's *Kashmir* off the Isle of Islay, and it continued to be managed independently by Anderson, Green & Company for more than 40 years.

P&O and Orient both had fleets to rebuild. The Orient Line initially acquired three liners, from the British Shipping Controller, which had been surrendered by Germany at the end of the war. Two passenger liners had been on order for P&O since 1914, and these were delivered in 1920. Additionally nine freighters were built between 1919 and 1921 and two former German cargo vessels were allocated to the Company. Although a number of ships were still under government control, by the end of 1921 weekly services to India, fortnightly to China and four weekly to Australia had been reintroduced.

Five new 13,000 ton liners for the Branch service were deployed between 1921 and 1922, and these were followed by the 16,000 ton *Moldavia* and *Mongolia* and the 20,000 ton *Mooltan* and *Maloja* for the direct Australian route in 1923 and 1924. The 15,000 ton *Cathay*, *Comorin* and *Chitral* (for the Australia service) and the 17,000 ton

The **Strathnaver** of 1931 was only the second P&O ship to feature a permanent white hull. She operated principally between London and Australia. (William Mayes collection)

Ranpura, *Ranchi*, *Rawalpindi* and *Rajputana* (for the Indian route) joined the fleet in 1925. During the latter half of the decade the Orient Line took delivery of a class of five 20,000 tonners.

The Company commenced cruising again in 1925, when the *Ranchi* undertook a Norwegian cruise as her maiden voyage. In the 1929 season P&O offered 15 cruises, including some on board the new *Viceroy of India*, and by 1932 both P&O and Orient Line were undertaking cruises from Australia, and tourist class cruises were begun in Europe.

The Branch service via the Cape was discontinued in 1929, although the ships continued to offer the third class service via Suez for a few more years.

The trade to Australia had by now become more important than that to India. During the 1930's P&O took delivery of the famous White Sisters, the five "Straths", which decreased the voyage time to Australia, and greatly increased the levels of comfort for passengers. These were the first class of P&O liners to feature permanent white hulls and buff funnels. Orient Line introduced two new ships with corn coloured hulls in place of the previously standard black. P&O and Orient were now coordinating their new-building programmes, though their ships looked very different.

The combined fleets had peaked in the mid 1920's at about 500 ships, ranging from the coasters and excursion ships of General Steam Navigation (acquired in 1920), to the modern refrigerated cargo ships of New Zealand Shipping Company and Federal Steam, and the state of the art passenger liners of P&O and Orient. Further companies were taken over, including Strick Line, Moss Hutchison, Asiatic Steam and Mogul Line, but all of this rebuilding work was, however, in vain as just around the corner was another, and altogether far more destructive war. P&O had 36 ships at the outbreak of the Second World War, 28 of which were passenger liners, and Orient Line had 8. Again, ships from both companies were called upon to serve as armed merchant cruisers, troopships and hospital ships. Although other ships served, and many were lost, one of the better known losses was that of the P&O armed merchant cruiser *Rawalpindi* in November 1939, following an engagement with the German battle cruisers *Scharnhorst* and *Gneisenau* to the south east of Iceland.

Among the 19 ships lost by P&O were the following passenger ships, listed chronologically: *Rawalpindi*, *Rajputana*, *Cathay*, *Viceroy of India*, *Narkunda*, *Ettrick*, and the *Strathallan*. Orient Line lost the *Orford*, *Orama*, *Oronsay* and the almost new *Orcades*. Other companies within the group lost a further 156 vessels.

By the end of the war commercial aviation was becoming viable over longer distances and sea mail contracts were discontinued, so this time there was not the need to replace passenger ship war losses on a one for one basis. Larger and faster ships were perceived to be the answer, but running less frequently. The combined P&O and Orient new-building programme was for a total of nine passenger ships but this was subsequently reduced to seven. In November 1945, P&O ordered two new liners, the *Himalaya* for the Australian run and the *Chusan* to serve the Far East, and shortly afterwards Orient placed an order for the *Orcades*. With many ships still in government service, passenger sailings to Australia did not recommence until February 1947 (Orient) and July 1947(P&O), with the latter's first sailing taken by the *Stratheden*. The *Canton* reopened the Far East service in October, but it was not until 1951 that the last liners, the *Strathnaver*, *Strathmore* and *Carthage* were handed back to the Company.

The new liners of the late 1940's and early 1950's (*Himalaya*, *Chusan*, *Iberia* and *Arcadia* for P&O and *Orcades*, *Oronsay* and *Orsova* for Orient) were able to reduce the voyage time to Australia from five to four weeks. The *Chusan* was the first major passenger liner to be fitted with Denny Brown stabilisers.

The cargo side of the business saw seven new and four secondhand ships join the fleet between 1945 and 1947, and by the end of 1949 the cargo fleet had been restored to pre-war strength.

Cruising began again in 1950 with a Mediterranean cruise undertaken by the new *Chusan*, before she entered service in the Far East trade. Cruising was still seen as a way of utilising ships when the liner business was slack.

In November 1955 Orient Line and P&O each ordered a large fast ship. At 27 knots the *Oriana*, 42,000 tons and the *Canberra*, 45,000 tons reduced the passage time to Australia to three weeks, when they entered service in 1960 and 1961 respectively. These were the largest

*The **Chusan** arriving in Southampton towards the end of her career.* (William Mayes collection)

ships ever built for this trade, and were the last to be built for the two companies' traditional liner services. On trials, speeds well in excess of the required service speed were achieved, with the *Oriana* at 30.64 knots almost one and a half knots faster than the *Canberra*. Upon the arrival of these ships, which were too big for the lock at Tilbury, the Australian service moved back to Southampton.

The 1960's saw major changes in the passenger trades. P&O acquired the remaining shares in Orient Line in 1960, and the passenger operation was restyled P&O-Orient Lines. Sailing frequencies were reduced, and the remainder of the pre-war liners

*The 1954 built **Arcadia** is seen here outward bound from the U.K. to Australia. (FotoFlite)*

were scrapped or sold. Trans-Pacific services were developed and two former Belgian passenger cargo liners were purchased to maintain the Far East service as *Cathay* and *Chitral*, but by the end of the decade, with closure of the Suez Canal, these had been transferred to the Australia-Japan route of subsidiary Eastern and Australian Steamship Company. The Far East route closed in 1969 and the *Chusan* made a last call at Bombay in 1970, leaving only the liner service to Australia and cruising as employment for the passenger fleet. The P&O-Orient title had been dropped in favour of P&O in the mid 1960's, and the corn coloured hulls of the Orient Line had all by then been replaced by P&O white.

The group's first tanker was Federal Steam's 18,000 dwt *Lincoln*, delivered in 1959. During the next year a further fourteen ships were delivered to P&O subsidiaries, including the *Garonne,* registered under the ownership of the Orient Steam Navigation Company. P&O itself owned few of these ships directly. To consolidate the position, Trident Tankers was set up in 1962, to manage and in most cases own the Group's tanker fleet. The operation of tankers during the 1970's and 1980's was a very volatile business, and P&O gradually reduced its tanker fleet, finally withdrawing from the market in 1992.

The first bulk-carrier for the group, the *Atherstone*, arrived in 1964, and along with seven similar ships was chartered to Associated Bulk Carriers, a joint P&O and Anglo Norness company. P&O later acquired a major stake in Anglo Norness, re-naming the company Anglo Nordic Shipping.

A year of enormous change is one way to describe 1971. The activities of more than 100 subsidiary companies were amalgamated into operating divisions within P&O. This meant that all of the cargo ships formerly operated by P&O and its subsidiaries were put into the General Cargo Division, the liners, along with BI's educational cruise

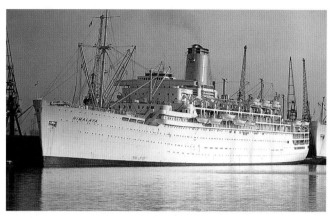

The first post-war liner for P&O was the **Himalaya**. (William Mayes collection)

ships *Uganda* and *Nevasa* formed the Passenger Division, and the tankers, bulk carriers and gas carriers became the fleet of the Bulk Shipping Division. Interestingly, the five BI passenger/cargo liners operating east of Suez were allocated to the General Cargo Division. From this time the ships of constituent companies flew the P&O flag and began to adopt a corporate identity.

Following this reorganisation the fleet consisted of 239 ships, including 136 general cargo liners, 27 coasters, 18 passenger liners, 17 ferries, 17 tankers and 6 bulk carriers.

The subsequent activities of the passenger, ferry, bulk carrier and container operations are dealt with elsewhere, so this chapter will conclude with a brief look at the other major events in the P&O story between 1971 and today. Union Steamship's 55 ships left the fleet at the end of that year when the company was sold, and in 1972 Strick Line's 17 ships joined the General Cargo Division on the acquisition by P&O of the remaining Strick shares. Cargo liner services now operated to and between India, Japan, Australia, New Zealand, the Indian Ocean, the Mediterranean and the Gulf.

The passenger trades in the Indian Ocean were in decline and the former BI ships were gradually withdrawn, the *Dwarka* being the last to go in 1982. Her demise ended a service going back 120 years for migrant labour from India to the Gulf. Her last glory was to be

*The **Uganda**, makes a triumphant return to Southampton in August 1982, at the end of her service in the Falklands War.* (William Mayes)

*The **Canberra** arrives in the Solent on her return from the Falklands War in 1982.* (FotoFlite)

featured as a P&O liner in the film "Gandhi".

During the 1970's a number of joint venture companies were set up. One of these was Panocean, formed in conjunction with Ocean Transport and Trading to operate a fleet of deep sea parcel tankers and coastal chemical tankers. Lauritzen Peninsular Reefers was another, running fast tramp refrigerated cargo ships.

In 1974-75 all the dry cargo ships were given new names, prefixed with 'Strath', repainted with biscuit coloured hulls and marketed as P&O Strath Services. However, with the containerisation and transfer of cargo trades to OCL, the general cargo fleet declined in numbers until in 1981 the remaining 31 'Straths' were combined with the Bulk Shipping Division to form a new Deep Sea Cargo Division. P&O closed its last conventional cargo service in 1982.

The 1970's were years of diversification away from shipping. A large network of road haulage operations was built up under the Ferrymasters, Pandoro, P&O Roadways and P&O Roadtanks names, and construction group Bovis was acquired in 1974.

Trafalgar House Investments mounted a hostile takeover bid for the Company in June 1983. By the time the Monopolies and Mergers Commission recommended that there should be no intervention, in March of the following year, Trafalgar were no longer interested in P&O. Jeffrey Sterling succeeded Lord Inchcape as chairman late in 1983, and shortly afterwards Sterling Guarantee Trust merged with P&O. By this time, with the diversity of the Group's interests, the shipping fleet had shrunk to just 42 ships.

The acquisition trail continued, with the takeover in 1986 of the remainder of Overseas Containers Limited, and property group Stock Conversion. The latter acquisition, when combined with other Group property interests put P&O into the UK's top three property investment and development groups. European Ferries became part of the group in January 1987, as did the Sitmar Cruises business in 1988. Later acquisitions included Rowbotham Tankships (subsequently sold) and most of the Ellerman Group's container shipping interests. On land the German haulage group Rhenania was incorporated into P&O European Transport Services, since renamed P&O Trans European.

As part of a strategy to concentrate more on its international businesses, P&O sold a large part of its UK industrial services division to the catering and leisure group Granada in 1993 (including Sutcliffe Catering, which had joined the Sterling Guarantee Trust Group in 1973). Further disposals of peripheral businesses followed as P&O moved its focus back towards shipping. By March 1999, the Group, including joint ventures and associates, was again a major force to be reckoned with in the shipping world, controlling some 276 ships.

At the same time Lord Sterling (as he had become) announced that it was his Board's intention to refocus the Group on the three core businesses: cruising, ferries, and ports and logistics. Disposal of property and service company interests began, and by early October almost one billion pounds had been realised from the sale of investment properties, Bovis Construction, Laing (Canada), service companies in Australia, and the London exhibition halls of Earls Court and Olympia. At the end of September, in line with declared strategy, but nonetheless taking the markets by surprise, it was announced that P&O, in conjunction with Arkona Touristik of Germany, had formed a new company under the name Aida Cruises to develop the German cruise market, now the second largest in Europe, taking over the existing cruise ship *Aida*, and subsequently ordering two new vessels.

It was known that P&O was prepared to move out of the container trades, by floating P&O Nedlloyd on the stock-market, but the announcement on 3rd February 2000 that the Company would de-merge its cruise businesses was a total surprise. This new cruise company, currently bearing the working name P&O Princess, will incorporate the cruising activities of P&O Cruises, Princess Cruises, P&O Australia, Swan Hellenic and Aida Cruises. More recently, a proposal to offer a majority of the shares in Associated Bulk Carriers has also been announced.

Without doubt, the remaining P&O group, focused on ports, ferries and logistics will be well placed to face the challenges of the new century.

*The **European Seaway** outward bound from Zeebrugge. The **Arcadia** can be seen on the inner mole at the port. (Mike Louagie)*

CHAPTER 2

P&O Cruises

The newly formed P&O Passenger Division inherited an ageing fleet of 13 liners in 1971, most of which had been designed and built for the passenger trade to Australia. The relaxation of air charter rules that year, and the advent of the Boeing 747 "Jumbo Jet" had signalled the end of line voyages to Australia, and within a year the passenger fleet had been redeployed to cruising in the UK, USA and Australian markets, with line voyages now only taking place when it was necessary to reposition a ship.

In 1971, the passenger liner fleet recorded its first financial loss for ten years, and the withdrawal of the 1954 built *Iberia* was announced early in 1972. However, there was some good news; the first new passenger ship for eleven years, the 17,000 ton *Spirit of London* entered the fleet in November as a running mate for the 18-year-old *Arcadia*, based in San Francisco. The *Spirit of London* had been bought off the stocks from an Italian shipyard, and was a near sister to Kloster's *Southward*.

Rationalisation continued with the *Chusan* and *Orcades* making their final voyages in 1973, and being sold for scrap. The *Canberra* almost met the same fate, as her season on the US East Coast had been a financial disaster. Various options were considered, including replacing her engines, selling her for further service or even scrapping her. Eventually, she was reprieved and the 20-year-old *Orsova* was scrapped instead, early in 1974.

The current Arcadia. (P&O)

At this time, the P&O Passenger Division fleet consisted of the *Nevasa* and *Uganda* (educational cruises), the *Arcadia* and *Spirit of London* (West Coast USA), the *Canberra*, *Himalaya*, *Oriana* and *Oronsay* (UK and Australia), and the *Cathay* and *Chitral* (Australia to Japan).

The passenger fleet continued to contract. The *Spirit of London* was transferred to the newly acquired Princess Cruises in October 1974, and the *Himalaya*, which had been based in Australia, was sold for scrapping later the same year, her place being taken by the *Arcadia*. Further withdrawals followed, with the *Oronsay*, *Chitral* and *Nevasa* leaving for the breakers and the *Cathay* being sold to the Chinese for further trading in 1975. P&O was not alone in disposing of its passenger ships, as most other liner operators were scrapping ships for which they could not find profitable employment. It was generally thought at this time that the day of the large passenger ship had gone forever. Who, then, could have predicted the way the cruise industry would develop, and the size of ships being built a mere quarter of a century later?

The general pattern of operation throughout the late 1970's was that the *Canberra* and *Oriana* serviced the mainstream UK cruising market with the *Uganda* providing educational cruises for school children and up to 300 adventurous adult passengers. The *Arcadia* was based permanently in Australia, assisted by the *Oriana* for a short season each year. The *Canberra* commenced what became a tradition of world cruises, leaving Southampton early in the new year with her 1975 sailing, a role that she continued until her withdrawal in 1997. Reflecting the changed nature of the business, in 1977 the P&O Passenger Division was restyled P&O Cruises.

By 1978, the *Arcadia* was approaching 25 years of age and would shortly need to be replaced. At that time a new ship for the Australian market was not an economic proposition, and so after a search for suitable second-hand tonnage the former Swedish America Line trans-Atlantic liner *Kungsholm* was acquired from Flagship Cruises. After a major refit, which included the removal of her forward funnel and the extension of the survivor, the newly renamed *Sea Princess* entered service in February 1979. The *Arcadia* was then sold to Taiwanese ship-breakers. The *Sea Princess* continued to serve the Australian cruise market until the spring of 1982, when she was transferred to the UK, her place being taken by the *Oriana*, which left Southampton for the last time in November 1981. An older and more traditional ship, better suited to Australian tastes, the *Oriana* served the Australian cruise market until March 1986, when she was sold to Japanese interests to become a conference centre at Beppu Bay. More recently she has been sold again and is now in China. Her place was taken seasonally by the *Island Princess,* which then spent six months in Australian waters and six months on her usual Princess duties. It was to be another two years before P&O had a year-round cruising programme in Australia again.

Towards the end of her world cruise, on 5th April 1982, the *Canberra* was requisitioned and transferred to the control of the Royal Navy to serve in the Falklands War. On arriving in Southampton two days later, she was refitted within 60 hours to carry 3,000 troops, together with their equipment and supplies. Helicopter pads were fitted over the forward open deck, and over the mid-ships swimming pool. This meant that additional strengthening steelwork had to be fitted in the public rooms below these areas. On 10th April she left Southampton bound for the South Atlantic and

*The first **Oriana** preparing to sail from Southampton around 1980.* (William Mayes)

war. Unlike the *Queen Elizabeth 2*, which was kept away from the battle zone, the *Canberra* spent some time at the very heart of the fighting in San Carlos Water, and although she came under attack from Argentinean aircraft she was not hit. Following the Argentinean surrender, the *Canberra* loaded more than 4,000 prisoners and ferried them to Puerto Madryn in Argentina, before loading troops in the Falklands and sailing for home. She arrived back in Southampton to a tumultuous welcome on 11th July 1982, and after a two-month refit resumed her cruising schedule on 11th September.

The *Uganda* was instructed to terminate her cruise early at Naples and sail to Gibraltar for conversion to a hospital ship on 10th April. Following a 65-hour stay in Gibraltar she proceeded south via Ascension. Following her return to Southampton in August, she was sent to the Tyne for refit, and on 25th September briefly resumed her normal duties. However, in the following January she was chartered to the Ministry of Defence for two years to run between Ascension and Port Stanley, while the new Falklands airport was completed. This effectively ended the BI educational cruise programme for all time, as schools, which normally planned trips two years ahead, had no guarantee that the ship would be available. At the end of her charter the *Uganda* spent some months laid up in the River Fal before going for breaking under the name of *Triton*.

The *Canberra* was marketed as P&O Cruises, and the *Sea Princess* as P&O Princess Cruises during 1982 and 1983. Later, cruises were advertised under the banners of Canberra Cruises and Sea Princess Cruises. Both ships served the UK market until the end of the 1986 season, when, due to reduced demand as a result of recession, the *Sea Princess* was transferred to Princess Cruises, for cruising in the Caribbean and to Alaska. The *Canberra* was then left to serve the needs of P&O's UK cruising passengers on her own. The *Sea Princess* returned to the UK during the summer of 1991 when new ships joined Princess Cruises, and these two ships then served the most rapidly expanding cruise market in the world until 1995.

When P&O acquired Sitmar in 1988, they also gained a ship which did not fit in with the rest of the Princess fleet, but which had developed a great following in Australia. The 22,000 ton *Fairstar*, delivered from Fairfield's in 1957 as Bibby Line's troopship *Oxfordshire*, not only retained her name (the only Sitmar Ship to do so) but was also initially marketed under the P&O-Sitmar banner.

The most significant event of the 1990's for the UK cruise industry was not the entry into the market of mass tour operators, but the introduction of the *Oriana*, the first ship to be purpose-built for the British cruise passenger. P&O had come in for criticism when, in 1982, the order for the *Royal Princess* went to a Finnish shipyard, but there can sadly be no doubt that neither then nor when the 69,000 ton *Oriana* was ordered from Jos L.

*The elegant **Victoria** (built in 1966) is now the smallest ship in the P&O Cruises fleet.* (P&O)

Meyer at Papenburg in Germany in 1992, was any British yard capable of building such a ship. She is based to a degree on the layout of the previous generation of ocean liner, and in particular the tremendously popular *Canberra*, although very much updated both in quality and range of facilities, to take into account the requirements of the modern British cruise passenger. Her interior has rightly been described as 'being in a timeless style but with classical taste'. Her cruising speed of 24 knots made her the fastest passenger ship to be built for a quarter of a century.

The *Oriana* was named in Southampton in April 1995 by Her Majesty Queen Elizabeth II and was an immediate success, despite some initial problems with vibration. With her tasteful and elegant interiors and

When delivered in 1961, the *Canberra* was hailed as 'the ship that shaped the future.' A quarter of a century later her modern lines still made her an impressive sight. (FotoFlite)

magnificent open decks (the largest area of an open deck on any cruise ship at the time) she became the ship by which all others were measured, not only in Europe but further afield. Her normal capacity of around 1,800 passengers gives her a higher passenger space ratio (39) than any other ship operating regularly from the UK. (Passenger Space Ratio is a relatively new way of assessing the amount of room per passenger, based on a calculation involving tonnage and lower bed capacity). Her introduction gave further impetus to an already fast growing cruise market in the UK.

Meanwhile, the *Sea Princess* had been renamed *Victoria* in March 1995, serving the dual purpose of freeing the name for future use by Princess Cruises, and giving the ship a name more in keeping with her partners in the P&O Cruises (UK) fleet.

In winter 1995/6 and 1996/7 the *Canberra* and *Oriana* each took a world cruise from Southampton, sailing round the world in opposite

The Arcadia joined the P&O Cruises fleet late in 1997 (P&O)

directions. This latter cruise was to be the *Canberra's* last, as she was now becoming very old, and the cost of bringing her up to current standards was prohibitive. Her retirement was announced in 1996, and for her 1997 season she was running at full capacity. She was withdrawn after her final cruise at the end of September 1997, and within days had quietly slipped off to Pakistani ship-breakers. The old ship had a last trick in her locker, however, for the breakers failed to run her as far up the beach as they really needed, and cutting her up offshore took much longer (and cost much more) than anyone had expected, not least because of the quality of her construction by Harland and Wolff.

P&O needed a modern vessel to replace the *Canberra* and found a suitable candidate from within the Princess fleet, the *Star Princess*. Built in France in 1989 and originally to have carried the name *Sitmar Fairmajesty*, she was the last ship to be launched for Sitmar. Tilburg Design were

Curzon Room - Oriana . (P&O)

contracted to redesign the interiors as far as possible to suit British tastes, and in December 1997, she commenced a new chapter in her career as P&O Cruises' *Arcadia*.

During 1996, the *Fairstar* suffered a number of breakdowns and it was decided to replace her early in 1997 with the *Fair Princess,* which had been laid up for some months following a failed sale to Regency Cruises. She underwent a six-month refit in San Diego, which brought her up to current SOLAS requirements. The *Fair Princess* (surprisingly not renamed) began her new career cruising in Australian waters in February 1997, sporting the plain buff P&O funnel, although managed by Princess Cruises on behalf of P&O Australia. She is due to be transferred from Australian cruising to New Zealand waters in October 2000, and her place should be taken by the 1984 built *Sky Princess*, to be renamed, somewhat unimaginatively, *Pacific Sky*.

As widely anticipated, in April 1997 P&O Cruises announced their order for a second new ship for the UK market, to enter service in May 2000. At 76,000 tons, the new *Aurora*, 40% of whose cabins feature balconies, will be about ten metres longer than the *Oriana*, and slightly wider above the promenade deck. Her PSR will be more than 41, which will put her alongside some of the new five star ships in that respect. It was entirely logical that, following the success of the *Oriana*, the new order should also go to Meyer Werft. She was floated out of her building dock in January 2000, and is due to make her first appearance in Southampton on 16th April. She will be named by The Princess Royal on 27th April and will depart on her maiden voyage on 1st May.

Even before the delivery of the *Aurora*, an order was placed for yet another new ship for the British market, this time with Fincantieri in Italy. Having essentially the same hull form as the *Grand Princess*, this 110,000 ton, 2,600 passenger giant is due to come into service in 2004 and operate fly cruises for British and European passengers in the Mediterranean and Caribbean.

*The **Oriana's** Riviera Pool, one of three, seen from the Sun Deck.* (John Hendy)

In a press release at the beginning of February 2000, it was announced that the cruise businesses of P&O are to be de-merged into a new company, currently bearing the working name P&O Princess. P&O Cruises (UK) will form the second largest element in this new entity.

The number of cruises available to passengers on the ships of P&O cruises in 2000 will be the highest ever offered at just over 100, excluding the separate sale of cruise segments, and as Princess are now also operating up to four ships in Europe each summer, it will be interesting, in the coming years, to see whether the European cruise business can continue to develop at a rate which will keep this growing fleet of ships profitably employed.

*The new **Aurora** makes her way slowly down the River Ems, heading for the open sea and her trials in February 2000. (P&O)*

The Oriana, dressed overall, at Trondheim in July 1998. (Richard Mayes)

P&O

P&O

	Aurora		Oriana
Gross tons	76,152	Gross tons	69,153
Net	40,037	Net	36,829
Deadweight	7,000	Deadweight	6,715
Length (o.a.)	270.00m	Length (o.a.)	260.00m
Breadth (Extr.)	32.24m	Breadth (Extr.)	32.24m
Draught (max)	7.90m	Draught (max)	8.20m
Passenger capacity	Normal 1,874/Maximum 1,950	Passenger capacity	Normal 1,822/Maximum 1,928
Cabins	934	Cabins	914
Builders	Meyer, Papenburg, Germany	Builders	Meyer, Papenburg, Germany
Yard No	640	Yard No	636
Built	2000	Built	1995
Entered service with P&O	2000	Entered service with P&O	1995
Engines	4 MAN B&W Diesels	Engines	4 MAN B&W Diesels
Speed (knots)	24.0	Speed (knots)	24.0
Call sign	GUSS	Call sign	GVSN
Cruise Area	UK, Europe, Worldwide	Cruise Area	UK, Europe, Worldwide
Crew	850	Crew	794
Flag	UK	Flag	UK

P&O

Gross tons	63,524	Gross tons	28,891
Net	32,185	Net	11,005
Deadweight	7,505	Deadweight	5,572
Length (o.a.)	245.60m	Length (o.a.)	201.23m
Breadth (Extr.)	32.23m	Breadth (Extr.)	26.57m
Draught (max)	8.15m	Draught (max)	8.56m
Passengers	Normal 1,448/Maximum 1,531	Passengers	Normal 704/Maximum 782
Cabins	735	Cabins	389
Builders	Chantiers de l'Atlantique, St Nazaire, France	Builders	John Brown, Glasgow, UK
Yard No	B29	Yard No	728
Built	1989	Built	1966
Entered service with P&O	1989	Entered service with P&O	1979
Engines	4 MAN B&W Diesels	Engines	2 Gotaverken Diesels
Speed (knots)	21.5	Speed (knots)	21.5
Call sign	GRFP	Call sign	GBBA
Cruise Area	UK, Europe, Caribbean	Cruise Area	UK, Europe, Caribbean
Crew	650	Crew	436
Flag	UK	Flag	UK
Former Names	*Star Princess, Sitmar FairMajesty*	Former Names	*Sea Princess, Kungsholm*

CHAPTER 3

Princess Cruises

Princess Cruises commenced operation in December 1965, when Stanley McDonald, a Seattle industrialist, chartered the 1949 built Canadian Pacific Railway ship, *Princess Patricia*, from which the new company took its name. This 6,000 ton, 347 berth ship, which had been converted from a ferry to a cruise-ship in 1963, proved to be so successful with her cruises to the Mexican West Coast from Los Angeles that the charter was renewed for the 1966/67 season. However, with increasing demand a larger ship was required for the following season, and a search found the

Royal Princess. (P&O)

12,000 ton, 467 passenger, *Italia*, which had just been completed at Trieste for a Sardinian ship owner, but which was available for charter. She took the name *Princess Italia* (for marketing purposes only), and began sailings to Mexico on 16th December 1967. With growing popularity a second ship was needed, and Costa Line's newly acquired and rebuilt *Carla C* commenced charter to Princess in December 1968. The arrival of the 20,000 ton *Princess Carla* (as she was marketed, but never named) allowed the *Italia* to inaugurate summer cruises to Alaska in 1969. The two ships maintained these schedules until the autumn of 1970 when the *Carla C* was recalled by Costa Line to replace a ship lost by fire. The *Italia* was then left on her own to run cruises to Mexico in winter, Alaska in summer and single Caribbean trips in the spring and autumn of 1971 and 1972.

A replacement for the *Carla C* was required, and the 20,000 ton *Island Venture*, unexpectedly available for charter, was the ideal solution. She began operating for Princess Cruises in September 1972 under the name *Island Princess*. She had been delivered in January that year as the *Island Venture*, joining her 1971-built sister the *Sea Venture*, to Norwegian Cruise ships, a company jointly formed by two Norwegian shipping companies, Fearney & Eger and Lorentzen for charter to Flagship Cruises for their new service from New York to Bermuda. Unfortunately, the service could not sustain two ships and the *Island Venture* was withdrawn and put back on the charter market.

In early 1973 the *Italia* ventured as far south as Rio de Janeiro, before being returned to her owners, thus leaving Princess Cruises again with a single ship.

By 1974 P&O was examining ways to expand its operation on the West Coast of the USA, but it was becoming increasingly difficult to compete with the new cruise companies with their modern purpose built tonnage. The Company's two ships, the *Spirit of London* and the *Arcadia*, while reasonably successful were hardly the ideal pairing. The way forward seemed to be the purchase of an established operator. Princess Cruises, which had gained a good reputation for quality, was perceived as an ideal candidate, so in August 1974 P&O bought out Princess, and

The Sun Princess, formerly Spirit of London, at Vancouver in 1981. (William Mayes collection)

shortly afterwards purchased the *Island Princess*. She was transferred from the Norwegian Registry to that of the United Kingdom, and her Norwegian complement was replaced by a British crew. In October 1974 P&O arranged to purchase the *Sea Venture* from Lorentzen, with delivery in April of the following year, at which time she took the name *Pacific Princess*.

The *Spirit of London* was transferred to the Princess fleet in late 1974, as the *Sun Princess*, and in December of that year Princess Cruises became the marketing name of P&O in North America. The *Arcadia* did not fit into this new fleet and she was permanently relocated to Australia. In 1975, with its three modern purpose built cruise ships, the operating pattern was set for Princess ships to cruise to Mexico and the South Pacific in the Northern Hemisphere's winter, and to Alaska in summer. This pattern was repeated for a number of years, although the *Pacific Princess* also spent some time cruising from Australia.

The growing US cruise market received a further boost in the late 1970's when the *Pacific Princess* took a starring role in the American TV soap opera series 'The Love Boat', which undoubtedly helped to increase the popularity of Princess Cruises in the USA, although it failed to have the same effect in the UK.

In February 1982 P&O announced its order for a 40,000 ton cruise ship, to be built in Finland, for the Princess fleet. The *Royal Princess*, as she was to become, was the largest purpose built cruise ship to be ordered to date, and in an innovative move, she was the first large passenger ship to feature all outside cabins. The new ship was duly delivered at the end of October 1984, and following a ten day visit to Southampton, was named there by Diana, Princess of Wales on 15th November. Following her inaugural Atlantic crossing, the *Royal Princess* took up her duties in North America and was not seen again in Europe until the late 1980's.

A decline in UK passengers, due to recession, led in 1986 to the *Sea Princess* being re-deployed to the Caribbean and Alaska, giving Princess its

*The **Fairsky** of 1984, later renamed **Sky Princess**, is seen in Sitmar livery at Fort Lauderdale in 1988.* (Ted Scull)

largest fleet to date, comprising the "Island", "Pacific", "Royal", "Sea" and "Sun" Princesses.

By 1988, it was apparent that P&O was once again falling behind the market leaders as the US cruise market boomed. P&O had no new ships on order, and only one really modern state of the art cruise ship in service. Other lines were preparing to take delivery of next generation ships of up to 70,000 tons. The solution again seemed to be the acquisition of another company, but this time it was the ships on order, which were of most interest.

Sitmar Line had been left virtually leaderless following the death of Boris Vlasov, the son of its founder, Alexandre Vlasov. This problem was compounded by financial difficulties caused by escalating costs and building delays with the three 60-70,000 ton cruise ships, which were on order. P&O made an offer to buy the Sitmar business in July 1988 for $210 million, which was accepted, and the takeover was completed on 1st September 1988.

Sitmar Line began trading just after the Second World War using two surplus US Government Victory liners which had been converted by the company to carry 800 passengers in fairly basic accommodation. Initial sailings were in the migrant trades between the Mediterranean and Venezuela outward, and the West Indies and England homebound. By 1949 a third ship was in operation, serving the emigrant trade from the UK to Australia. Later, this ship, the *Fairsea* inaugurated Sitmar's full passenger service between Europe and Australia. A fourth ship, British India's 1930 built *Kenya*, was acquired in 1952 and re-named *Castel Felice*. The Australian Government's introduction of the £10 assisted passage scheme in 1958 prompted the conversion of a cargo ship, which Sitmar had purchased seven years earlier, into the 1,600 passenger *Fairsky*. A last acquisition in this era was the former Bibby Line troopship *Oxfordshire*, which was refurbished and given the name *Fairstar* in 1963. She was intended for UK cruising, but did not prove popular. However, she found her niche cruising from Australian ports, a role she performed for almost 30 years.

In the late 1960's Sitmar, intending to give a boost to the now declining Australian migrant trades, had purchased two former Cunard liners, the 1956-built *Carinthia* and the one year younger *Sylvania,* with a view to converting them for a high quality emigrant service. However, at this time the Australian Government awarded the new contract to the Greek Chandris Line, and Sitmar were left with two ships and no work for them. The Vlasovs then took the bold step of having these liners converted into luxury cruise ships for the North American market, where they began sailing in 1971. The *Carinthia* became the *Fairsea* and was positioned at Fort Lauderdale, while the *Sylvania*, renamed *Fairwind,* cruised from San

The Island Princess at San Francisco during 1998, her last season with Princess Cruises. (Andrew Kilk)

Francisco to Alaska in summer and from Los Angeles to Mexico in winter.

With two of the most luxurious ships afloat, Sitmar Cruises, as the Company was now styled, quickly built up an enviable reputation for quality, and was soon operating at full capacity. By 1980 expansion plans were being considered, and it was decided to convert the 1961 built former Portuguese liner *Principe Perfeito* for luxury cruising. The idea was eventually dropped in favour of building a new ship, the first new-building for the company. The new *Fairsky* was built in France, and surprisingly the mode of propulsion chosen was steam turbines (probably the last large passenger ship to be so powered). When she was delivered in 1984, although the world's largest cruise ship, and larger by 2,000 tons than the *Royal Princess*, she was eclipsed by that ship's modern profile and innovatory features.

The phenomenal growth in cruise holidays continued, and in 1986 Sitmar ordered another new ship from the French shipyard Chantiers de l'Atlantique. At 63,000 tons she was floated out as the *Sitmar FairMajesty*, but was never to sail under that name as she was acquired by P&O before completion and given the name *Star Princess*. Two further ships of 70,000 tons were later ordered from Fincantieri in Italy, and these too were eventually delivered to Princess Cruises.

The bulk of the former Sitmar fleet, comprising the *Fair Princess* (ex *Fairsea*), *Sky Princess* (ex *Fairsky*) and *Dawn Princess* (ex *Fairwind*) was merged into the Princess Cruises operation in time for the 1989 season. The *Fairstar* remained in Australia under that name, and ownership passed to P&O. In March 1989, the arrival of the first of the Sitmar new-buildings, now named *Star Princess* allowed the *Sun Princess*, the smallest ship in the fleet, to be withdrawn and sold to Premier Cruise Lines in May.

In July 1990, the first of the two new 1,600 passenger berth cruise-ships ordered by Sitmar was delivered carrying the name *Crown Princess*. At 70,000 tons she was at that time the largest such ship ever built for P&O, and for a short while the largest operational passenger ship in the world. Together with her sister, the *Regal Princess*, she was the first major passenger ship to be built in Italy for almost 25 years, and thus began a relationship with Fincantieri, which has continued with Princess to the present day, and helped to establish Fincantieri as one of the four leading cruise-ship builders in the world.

By now Princess Cruises had truly become a global operator, and a look at the 1990 brochure reveals just how many areas of the world were covered by this fine fleet of nine ships. The newest member of the fleet, the *Crown Princess* began her service in the Mediterranean in July, before moving to the Caribbean in October. The "Dawn", "Fair", "Island" and "Pacific" Princesses spent the summer on two week Alaska cruises, with two departures a week from both Anchorage and Vancouver, and during the rest of the year they all spent some time cruising in the Caribbean. All but the *Pacific Princess* cruised to Mexico, but she undertook cruises to Rio de Janeiro, and Manaus, more than a thousand miles up the River Amazon. The *Star Princess* was also based in Vancouver for the summer, performing seven day itineraries to Glacier Bay, and in Fort Lauderdale for Caribbean service in winter. The *Sea Princess* spent much of the year operating in the Pacific from Australia, Singapore and Hong Kong, with positioning voyages between Japan and Vancouver, and a short summer season cruising to Alaska from San Francisco. The *Sky Princess* operated cruises in the Caribbean and from New York to Montreal. The *Royal Princess* spent much of the summer in the Mediterranean and Baltic, and other months in the Caribbean, with several transits of the Panama Canal to and from Acapulco.

The last of the Sitmar new-buildings, the *Regal Princess* was delivered in August 1991, and in anticipation of her arrival the *Sea Princess* was despatched back to the UK in time for the summer season. Fleet deployment over the next few years continued much along the lines outlined above, but with an increasing emphasis on European cruises.

By 1993, the *Dawn Princess* was nearly forty years old, and she was sold to V-ships of Monaco (the former managers of Sitmar Line), to become their *Albatros*. Her replacement was the chartered 28,000 ton former *Royal Viking Sky*, which became *Golden Princess*.

Planning for the next new ship had begun around 1990, however, by the time that the $300 million *Sun Princess* entered service in December 1995 she had become the lead vessel of what has now turned out to be a series of four Fincantieri-built 77,000 ton super-liners. With a capacity for 1,950 passengers, her hull dimensions are the maximum possible for transiting the Panama Canal. Undoubtedly she and her sisters set the new standard for ships operating from North America.

The arrival of the *Sun Princess* released the now surplus *Fair Princess*, which was sold to Regency Cruises. However, the sale fell through when that company went into liquidation, and she was laid up by P&O in Mexico. Eventually refitted, she was transferred to P&O's Australian operation as a replacement for the *Fairstar*. Interestingly she was not renamed.

At the end of 1996 the charter of the *Golden Princess* expired and she was returned to her owners, in turn to be sold to Star Cruises as their *Superstar Capricorn*. Her replacement was the second of the *Sun Princess* class, the *Dawn Princess*, delivered early in 1997. The last members of this class are the *Sea Princess*, delivered late in 1998 and *Ocean Princess*, which entered service in February 2000.

The *Star Princess* was transferred to P&O cruises for operation out of Southampton in the autumn of 1997. Following a major internal refit she commenced service in December of that year under the name *Arcadia*.

The year 1998 was memorable for the arrival of the Fincantieri built *Grand Princess*, at that time the world's largest cruise ship at almost 109,000 tons. She carries 2,600 passengers in some 1,300 staterooms and has a complement of more than 1,100 crew members. Too large to transit the Panama Canal, the *Grand Princess* spends summers in the Mediterranean, and winters in the Caribbean. She has been a phenomenal success from the day that she was introduced, being fully booked to date. She has two sisters due for delivery in April 2001 and January 2002.

The new generation of large ships are currently being marketed as "Grand Class Cruising", with great emphasis on choice in dining and other shipboard activities, and therefore it was not surprising to learn that, in the spring of 1999, the (now small) *Island Princess* had been sold to Hyundai for cruising from South Korea. Perhaps more surprising was the announcement shortly afterwards that orders had been placed for four more ships for the Princess fleet, comprising a further two 110,000 ton *Grand Princess* types to be built by Mitsubishi in Japan (the first western cruise-ship order to be placed in that country), and two (the first of a new class?) 88,000 ton ships from Chantiers de l'Atlantique in France. The

*When delivered in 1998, the **Grand Princess** was the largest passenger ship ever built.* (P&O)

French-built ships will feature a combination of diesel and gas turbine engines, with the gas turbines located in the funnel. Not only does this make the ships more environmentally friendly, but it also generates more space inside the ship for additional facilities or cabins. Potentially these and the existing orders, now for a total of seven ships (with at least two further options) could double the capacity of the fleet by the time that they are all delivered by the end of 2004. However, there are three of the current fleet of nine ships, which do not really fit the "Grand Class" concept. The *Sky Princess* as a replacement for the *Fair Princess* (which will move to New Zealand) has already been allocated to the Australian

operation (managed by Princess on behalf of P&O Australia) with effect from the autumn of 2000, when she will be renamed *Pacific Sky*. The *Pacific Princess* and the *Royal Princess* are the other members of this trio. The *Royal Princess* is now a regular caller at UK ports as one of four Princess ships to operate in European waters during the summer, and we would like to think that, suitably renamed, she will be the eventual replacement for the *Victoria* in the UK market when that ship reaches her retirement.

A major announcement in February 2000 signalled the intention to de-merge the cruise businesses into a new company, of which Princess will constitute a major part. The new company, currently bearing the working name P&O Princess, will have as its chief executive Peter Ratcliffe (currently president of Princess Cruises), while Lord Sterling will take the role of chairman. To be quoted on the London and New York stock exchanges, P&O Princess will be headquartered in London.

*One of the luxury suites onboard the **Grand Princess**.* (P&O)

Gross tons	108,806
Net	73,238
Deadweight	6,750
Length (o.a.)	289.51m
Breadth (Extr.)	40.20m
Draught (max)	8.50m
Passengers	Normal 2,600/Maximum 3,330
Cabins	1296
Builders	Fincantieri, Monfalcone, Italy
Yard No	5956
Built	1998
Entered service with P&O	1998
Engines	6 Sulzer Diesels
Speed (knots)	22.5
Call sign	ELVG9
Cruise Area	Caribbean, Mediterranean
Crew	1,100
Flag	Liberia (Bermuda by December 2000)

P&O

P&O

Gross tons	77,441
Net	44,193
Deadweight	8,293
Length (o.a.)	261.31m
Breadth (Extr.)	32.28m
Draught (max)	8.10m
Passenger capacity	Normal 1,950/Maximum 2,272
Cabins	1008
Builders	Fincantieri, Monfalcone, Italy
Yard No	6044
Built	2000
Entered service with P&O	2000
Engines	4 Sulzer Diesels
Speed (knots)	21.5
Call sign	MZXH7
Cruise Area	Caribbean, Alaska
Crew	900
Flag	UK

Gross tons	69,845
Net	34,907
Deadweight	6,946
Length (o.a.)	245.08m
Breadth (Extr.)	32.28m
Draught (max)	8.10m
Passenger capacity	Normal 1,590/Maximum 1,672
Cabins	798
Builders	Fincantieri, Monfalcone, Italy
Yard No	5839
Built	1990
Entered service with P&O	1990
Engines	4 MAN Diesels
Speed (knots)	19.5
Call sign	ELVK5
Cruise Area	Caribbean, Scandinavia East Coast North America
Crew	671
Flag	Liberia (Bermuda by December 2000)

Gross tons	77,441		Gross tons	77,441
Net	44,193		Net	44,193
Deadweight	8,293		Deadweight	8,270
Length (o.a.)	261.31m		Length (o.a.)	261.31m
Breadth (Extr.)	32.28m		Breadth (Extr.)	32.28m
Draught (max)	8.10m		Draught (max)	8.11m
Passenger capacity	Normal 1,950/Maximum 2,272		Passenger capacity	Normal 1,950/Maximum 2,272
Cabins	999		Cabins	1,011
Builders	Fincantieri, Monfalcone, Italy		Builders	Fincantieri, Monfalcone, Italy
Yard No	5955		Yard No	5909
Built	1997		Built	1995
Entered service with P&O	1997		Entered service with P&O	1995
Engines	4 Sulzer Diesels		Engines	4 Sulzer Diesels
Speed (knots)	21.4		Speed (knots)	21.5
Call sign	ELT04		Call sign	MZFE8
Cruise Area	Caribbean/Alaska		Cruise Area	Panama, Caribbean, Alaska
Crew	900		Crew	900
Flag	Liberia (UK from May 2000)		Flag	UK

P&O

William Mayes

Gross tons	24,799
Net	12,228
Deadweight	6,742
Length (o.a.)	185.40m
Breadth (Extr.)	24.49m
Draught (max)	8.94m
Passenger capacity	Normal 890/Maximum 1,100
Cabins	481
Builders	John Brown, Glasgow, UK
Yard No	699
Built	1956
Entered service with P&O	1988
Engines	4 John Brown Steam Turbines
Speed (knots)	19.5
Call sign	ELMQ
Cruise Area	Australia
Crew	450
Flag	Liberia
Former Names	*Fairsea, Fairland, Carinthia*

Gross tons	20,186
Net	7,856
Deadweight	3,673
Length (o.a.)	168.74m
Breadth (Extr.)	24.64m
Draught (max)	7.70m
Passenger capacity	Normal 640/Maximum 717
Cabins	324
Builders	Rheinstahl Nordseewerke, Emden,Germany
Yard No	411
Built	1971
Entered service with P&O	1975
Engines	4 Fiat Diesels
Speed (knots)	19.0
Call sign	GBCF
Cruise Area	Africa, Mediterranean, Bermuda
Crew	350
Flag	UK
Former Name	*Sea Venture*

P&O

John Hendy

Gross tons	69,845
Net	34,907
Deadweight	6,946
Length (o.a.)	245.10m
Breadth (Extr.)	32.28m
Draught (max)	8.10m
Passenger capacity	Normal 1,590/Maximum 1,672
Cabins	798
Builders	Fincantieri, Monfalcone, Italy
Yard No	5840
Built	1991
Entered service with P&O	1991
Engines	4 MAN Diesels
Speed (knots)	19.5
Call sign	ELVK6
Cruise Area	Mexico,Alaska,Polynesia,FarEast,Australasia
Crew	671
Flag	Liberia (UK by May 2000)

Gross tons	44,588
Net	19,744
Deadweight	4,661
Length (o.a.)	230.61m
Breadth (Extr.)	29.20m
Draught (max)	7.80m
Passenger capacity	Normal 1,200/Maximum 1,260
Cabins	600
Builders	Wartsila, Helsinki, Finland
Yard No	464
Built	1984
Entered service with P&O	1984
Engines	4 Pielstick Diesels
Speed (knots)	21.5
Call sign	GBRP
Cruise Area	S America, Europe, Worldwide
Crew	520
Flag	UK

P&O

P&O

Gross tons	77,441		Gross tons	46,087
Net	44,193		Net	21,617
Deadweight	8,251		Deadweight	6,135
Length (o.a.)	261.31m		Length (o.a.)	240.39m
Breadth (Extr.)	32.28m		Breadth (Extr.)	27.84m
Draught (max)	8.10m		Draught (max)	8.17m
Passenger capacity	Normal 1,950/Maximum 2,272		Passenger capacity	Normal 1200/Maximum 1350
Cabins	1,008		Cabins	580
Builders	Fincantieri, Monfalcone, Italy		Builders	CNM, La Seyne, France
Yard No	5995		Yard No	1436
Built	1998		Built	1984
Entered service with P&O	1998		Entered service with P&O	1988
Engines	4 Sulzer Diesels		Engines	2GEC CNAV Steam Turbines
Speed	19.5		Speed (knots)	21.5
Call sign	MZLT8		Call sign	ELVD4
Cruise Area	Caribbean, Alaska, Hawaii		Cruise Area	Alaska then Australasia as *Pacific Sky*
Crew	900		Crew	550
Flag	UK		Flag	Liberia (UK by May 2000)
			Former Name	*Fairsky*

Aida Cruises

At the end of September 1999 it was announced that P&O and the German cruise operator Arkona Touristik had agreed to form a new company, Aida Cruises, to develop the German cruise business. In 1998 some 300,000 German passengers took ocean cruises, making that market the second largest (and second fastest growing) in Europe. It was anticipated that Aida Cruises would also encompass the activities of Arkona's subsidiary, Seetours International, together with its 18,000 ton cruise ship, the *Arkona*, giving it an estimated 25% share of the German cruise market, but this part of the deal had not been concluded at the time of writing..

Arkona Touristik is a subsidiary of Deutsche Seereederei, the former East German state shipping group, which is now owned privately by the Rahe family, following privatisation in 1993. Problems with its cargo ship operations forced the company to sell their single cruise ship, the 1996 built *Aida* in 1997 to raise finance. Norwegian Cruise Line was the buyer, and the ship was chartered back to Arkona, who re-acquired the ship in the summer of 1999.

The 38,000 ton *Aida*, which caters for the younger to middle age German passenger who prefer a premium quality, resort style holiday, has a passenger capacity of 1,186. Two further ships of similar style and capacity have now been ordered from Aker MTW Werft at Wismar, Germany. P&O's initial investment in the new company is DM150 million, and it holds 51% of the share capital, with options to acquire the remainder when the new ships enter service in 2002 and 2003.

Aida Cruises is expected to become part of the new cruise company towards the end of 2000.

P&O

Gross tons	38,531
Net	17,094
Deadweight	3,752
Length (o.a.)	193.34m
Breadth (Extr.)	32.60m
Draught (max)	6.20m
Passenger capacity	Normal and Maximum 1,186
Cabins	593
Builders	Kvaerner Masa Yards, Turku, Finland
Yard No	1337
Built	1996
Entered service with P&O	1999
Engines	4 MAN Diesels
Speed (knots)	18.5
Call sign	ELVB5
Cruise Area	Caribbean, Mediterranean
Crew	370
Flag	Liberia

CHAPTER 5

Swan Hellenic

The charter of the *Uganda* by P&O to the Ministry of Defence in early 1983, signalled not only the end of BI's educational cruise programme for schools, but also the specialist cultural cruises which were run in conjunction with it. The withdrawal of the school ship operation, sad though it was to see it finish, did not present a major problem, as the market had been declining for some years. However, the adults who had enjoyed the so-called 'Discovery Cruises' aboard the *Uganda* had no similar alternative within the P&O group. Fortunately this problem was short-lived as, during the

Minerva. (P&O)

course of 1983 the opportunity arose for P&O to buy the specialist tour operator W F & R K Swan (Hellenic) Ltd from its owners, Trust House Forte. Swans ran land-based art treasures tours, European river cruises, Nile cruises and, the jewel in its crown, Mediterranean cultural cruises aboard the *Orpheus*. Swans were renowned not only for the quality of their cruises and shore excursions (the price of which was generally included in the fare), but also for the outstanding lecturers that they were able to obtain to accompany their trips.

The origin of Swan Hellenic Cruises dates back to the 1930's when the Hellenic Travellers Club ran cruises and tours to Greece and Asia Minor. After the Second World War, Hellenic Cruises were begun again by W F & R K Swan who then owned the club. The first such cruise was undertaken in 1954 aboard the 1,700 ton, 1952 built *Miaoulis,* and during the second

cruise, in 1955, the most celebrated of Swan's guest lecturers, the archaeologist Sir Mortimer Wheeler, started his connection with the firm of which he later became Chairman. By the autumn of 1961, 27 of these cruises had been arranged, and a pattern of three early and three late season cruises aboard the *Ankara*, chartered from Turkish Maritime Lines, had emerged.

The number of cruises offered each year steadily increased, and by 1973 Swans had begun to look for a replacement for the 1927 built *Ankara*, which was only partly air conditioned, and certainly by then well past her best. They settled on the *Orpheus*, owned by the Greek operator, Epirotiki Steamship Navigation Company.

The *Orpheus* was launched in 1948 as the British and Irish Steam Packet Company's passenger ferry *Munster*. On her withdrawal from the Irish Sea in 1968 she was acquired by Epirotiki and renamed *Theseus*, a name under which she never traded. Over the course of the next two years the ship underwent a major refit from which she emerged as a splendid little cruise ship with 155 cabins, all of which had private facilities. The *Orpheus*, as she was now named, spent her first two years cruising for her owners from Seattle to Alaska, and from Los Angeles to Mexico. The following two years were spent cruising in the Mediterranean. Swans chartered her for the 1974 summer season, and that charter continued for a further 21 seasons.

Though the *Orpheus,* while under charter to Swans, spent most of her time in the Eastern Mediterranean, she did sometimes venture further afield to the Western Mediterranean, the Red Sea, and even to England in the early 1980's where she did a number of round Britain cruises. Her time off charter was usually spent in refit, cruising for her owners or, in later years, laid up.

When P&O bought Swans in 1983 they acquired a real gem in a loyal niche market, which at that time attracted a predominance of North American passengers. They kept the operation separate from the rest of their cruising activities, and continued to market the brand as Swan Hellenic, but the cruising season was very quickly extended to ten months each year. The ship continued, for the most part, to cruise in the Eastern Mediterranean,

The **Orpheus** *operated for Swan Hellenic from 1974 to 1995. She is seen here at Venice in 1974.* (William Mayes collection)

with occasional forays outside this area.

At the time of the takeover, the only other ship on long-term seasonal charter to Swans was the Nile cruiser *Nile Star,* of around 350 tons and with accommodation for some 70 passengers. She spent ten months each year on charter, cruising the 600 miles between Cairo and Luxor. Swans had entered the Nile cruise market as early as 1960. Around 1992 the *Nile Star* was replaced by the larger *Nile Monarch,* but terrorist activity in Egypt in later years dissuaded the (still predominantly) American passengers in particular from venturing to that part of the world. In later years a much-reduced programme has been offered aboard ships such as the *Nubian Sea* and *Vittoria,* but, sadly, Nile cruises no longer feature in Swan's programme.

Swans have continued to offer a selection of cruises aboard exclusively chartered vessels along the major waterways of Northern Europe, together with cruises from St. Petersburg to Moscow. For a while they were also involved in the marketing of the P&O Spice Island cruises in Indonesia, 50% owned by P&O Australia from 1990 to 1995. However, Swans continue to expand their horizons, and a recent development has been the introduction of Amazon River cruises, aboard the 120 passenger, *Clipper Adventurer.* A single successful cruise in 1999 has led to three such itineraries for 2000.

During the early 1990's P&O had begun to look for a replacement for the *Orpheus,* and eventually, in 1994, a contract was signed for a new ship. The Mariotti Shipyard in Genoa were to build a ship to be owned by V-Ships of Monaco (the former managers of Sitmar Line), and chartered for a minimum of four years by P&O. Mariotti, having insufficient facilities to build the hull, were intending to subcontract this work to another yard, but they found instead an almost complete hull at a shipyard in Nikolajev, Ukraine. This hull had been laid down by the Okean Shipyard in 1989 as a research vessel for the Russian fleet. Following the break-up of the Soviet Bloc, the order was cancelled and building work suspended. V-Ships acquired the unfinished hull, and after it had been completed to main deck level and launched in December 1994, had it towed to Genoa. In April 1996 the new *Minerva* entered service in the Mediterranean for Swans, and, two months later, while in London she was officially named by HRH The Duchess of Gloucester.

The *Minerva's* cruising programme is quite different from that undertaken by the *Orpheus*. In a typical year, the *Minerva* is in the Far East during winter, then makes her way to the Mediterranean during the spring, progressing into the Atlantic and up to The British Isles and Scandinavia for summer, before returning to the Mediterranean in autumn, and then back to Far Eastern destinations such as Sri Lanka, India, Indonesia and Vietnam for winter.

The *Orpheus*, which had been returned to her owners for further service at the end of the 1995 season, is remembered aboard the *Minerva*, where the conservatory is named The Orpheus Room. Traditionally, there is no fixed seating plan in the dining room, a flexible and informal arrangement that has proved extremely popular with passengers. The *Minerva* has several fine rooms, but among the most impressive must surely be her elegant, oak panelled library, stocked with more than 4,000 volumes, and, on the deck above, the intimate Wheeler Bar. In recent years the passenger mix has swung in favour of the British traveller, who now take some 50% of her capacity. The *Minerva*, now the sole ship operating permanently for Swans, is currently manned by British officers with Ukrainian and Filipino crew.

Swan Hellenic, to become part of the new de-merged cruise company, is now Europe's leading operator of expedition type cruises, and although the initial charter of *Minerva* is set to expire in the spring of 2000, with the great success she has been, her cruising days for Swan Hellenic should continue for many years to come.

William Mayes

Gross tons	12,331
Net	4,283
Deadweight	1,500
Length (o.a.)	133.00m
Breadth (Extr.)	20.00m
Draught (max)	5.08m
Passenger capacity	Normal 356/Maximum 474
Cabins	178
Builders	Okean Shipyard Ukraine and Mariotti, Genoa, Italy
Yard No	001/595
Built	1996
Entered service with P&O	1996
2 Pielstick	2 Pielstick Diesels
Speed (knots)	16.00
Call sign	C6NP5
Cruise Area	Europe, Middle East, SE Asia
Crew	157
Flag	Bahamas
Former Name	*Okean*

CHAPTER 6

P&O Stena Line

The alliance between P&O European Ferries and Stena Line, their former rivals on the Dover Strait, was formed in March 1998. The operation is wholly independent of both British and Swedish parent companies and as such should fall outside the scope of this present publication. It is however included for the sake of completeness and for the fact that the company and its ships use both the P&O name and livery (slightly modified), the P&O house flag is part of P&O Stena's identity, and P&O holds a 60% interest in the joint concern.

P&OSL Aquitaine. (John Hendy)

The ancestry of the P&O involvement goes back to 1928 when Mr. Stuart M. Townsend chartered the 368 ton collier *Artificer* for a brief summer season to offer motorists a cut-price motor car ferry service linking Dover with Calais. Townsend's original plan was to end the monopoly then enjoyed by the Southern Railway Company, undercut their fares by half and force them to reduce their rates after which he would withdraw. But his initial success saw a profit of £80 in the first season which prompted a further charter during 1929 after which the former minesweeper HMS *Ford* was purchased and converted for merchant use after being inspected at the scrap yard at Dover's Eastern Docks.

Renamed *Forde,* the eleven year old steamer commenced service in April 1930 carrying up to 168 passengers and 28 cars. She was an immediate success and throughout the 'thirties the family-owned 'Townsend Channel Ferry' blossomed.

Townsend had seen from an early time that the drive-on method of loading was the way ahead but the authorities on both sides of the Channel were reluctant to allow the construction of linkspans over which cars could be driven between ship and shore. The *Forde* was actually relaunched with a stern gate and when in June 1936 a French General Strike paralysed the cranes at Calais, she simply presented her stern to the quay and allowed her vehicles to drive directly onto French soil. All those who witnessed this historic occasion saw the foundations laid for a transport revolution.

Success continued after the war and the elderly *Forde* was sold for further service at Gibraltar. Her replacement was another former Royal Navy vessel, the River class frigate HMS *Halladale*. After her conversion at Cork, she took up service in April 1950 and in the following June opened the drive-on ramp at Calais although she was not able to use similar facilities at Dover until April 1953.

In 1956, continued growth prompted Townsend to go public but the share issue was launched on the very day that Nasser announced the nationalisation of the Suez Canal. Trade on the Stock Exchange slumped and few shares were sold.

At this time the Coventry-based Mr. George Nott and his associates were scouring the market looking for a small company with large assets which they could transfer to their own. A controlling interest in Townsend Bros. Car Ferries was duly secured after which the Townsend family's involvement eventually ceased.

It was initially Nott's intention to strip the ferry company of its assets and to wind-up the ferry service but sense prevailed and the *Halladale* continued to make handsome profits for her new owners.

The new regime was far more aggressive and now looked further afield than the traditionally seasonal car ferry traffic. Some of its ideas were very forward-looking and were amply illustrated when in 1959 a subsidiary company European Ferries was formed and the former tank-landing craft *Empire Shearwater* was taken on long-term charter to provide a service for lorries and heavy vehicles. Sadly the climate was not then right for such a link and after just six months it ended in failure.

The first of the well-known green-hulled ferries, the £1 million *Free Enterprise* entered service in April 1962 and was followed in May 1965 by the *Free Enterprise II* - the first British-registered drive-through ferry. She opened the Dover - Zeebrugge link in March 1966 after which time expansion, especially of freight, was tremendous and between 1966 and 1974 six more larger 'Free Enterprise' vessels were added to the fleet.

The year 1968 had seen the acquisition of the Norwegian-owned Thoresen Car Ferries after which the European Ferries Group was created and eventually the combined fleets adopted the orange hulls of the Thoresen ships. The enlarged company was the largest independent ferry concern in Europe and was further strengthened in 1971 by the purchase of the Atlantic Steam Navigation Company and in 1985 of P&O Normandy Ferries.

The continuing demand for freight space particularly on the Zeebrugge link saw the introduction of three 'European' class roll on - roll off freighters in 1975, 1976 and 1978. The *Free Enterprise VI* and *Free Enterprise VII* both underwent major surgery in 1985 when they were raised and lengthened to increase their lorry capacity from 24 to 60 units. The result was not a pretty

*From 1961 to 1974 Townsend Thoresen built a series of eight Free Enterprise class ships for their operations to Calais and Zeebrugge. The **Free Enterprise IV** is seen here leaving Boulogne for Dover in 1986.* (Miles Cowsill)

sight but this clever piece of engineering allowed two well-tried ships to continue their successful careers at a time when the cost of building replacements would have been prohibitive.

Some five years earlier the company had introduced a completely new generation of cross-Channel ferries. The *Spirit of Free Enterprise* and her two sisters offered 75 minute crossings which enabled as many as five daily round sailings to be operated between Dover and Calais by each ship. They were the first Channel ferries to be built with twin vehicle decks both capable of carrying freight. Such was the success of the concept that when plans for the present fixed cross Channel link were unveiled, Townsend Thoresen soon declared their intention of offering their own "Chunnel

In anticipation of the building of the Channel Tunnel, Townsend Thoresen built three Spirit class vessels for their Dover-Calais operation. The first of these vessels The **Spirit of Free Enterprise** *is seen here leaving Calais in 1981.* (Miles Cowsill)

Beaters' - twin giant ferries (with double the lorry capacity of the previous 'Spirit' class) which they claimed would threaten the financial viability of the tunnel.

The £85 million *Pride of Dover* and *Pride of Calais* both entered service during 1987 but prior to this (in January 1986) the P&O Group had acquired a controlling interest in a company holding almost 21% of the European Ferries Group shares. P&O Chairman Sir Jeffrey Sterling was invited to join the Board and from that time the future of the EFG was always in doubt. By this time the company had accrued large land holdings

in the United States where a drop in oil prices eventually brought the EFG to its knees. The Board invited P&O to act as their liferaft and this was duly accomplished in January 1987. The ferry division continued to trade as Townsend Thoresen but following the 'Herald' disaster off Zeebrugge in March, P&O acted decisively to distance themselves from the former regime and duly created P&O European Ferries in October 1987.

During 1991-93, four more vessels were added to the Dover-based fleet in the form of the three 'Super-European' class freighters for the Zeebrugge link and their half sister the *Pride of Burgundy* which entered service in April 1993. With the stretching of the *Pride of Kent* (formerly the *Spirit of Free Enterprise*) in June 1992, the P&O European Ferries fleet of superferries now numbered five. The fitting of Club Class and luxury lounges on all ships set a standard which was the envy of others and the company carried three times more traffic from Dover and Calais than their nearest competitor.

During the preparation for the opening of the tunnel, the secondary passenger routes to Zeebrugge (in December 1991) and Boulogne (in January 1993) were closed although Zeebrugge continues in a freight-only capacity. It was important that all efforts should be directed at the premier route against the tunnel and so services which might serve to weaken that position were terminated. As it was, P&O European Ferries had its own Channel Shuttle service up and running by summer 1993 a whole year and a half before the tunnel eventually opened.

The Stena side of the partnership holds a 40% stake in the present company. Stena Line of Gothenburg in Sweden took over the former Sealink fleet following a hostile takeover battle with Sea Containers in April 1990. Sealink had been de-nationalised and sold for just £66 million in July 1984 after which the company traded as Sealink British Ferries. No purpose-built tonnage was added to any route apart from those to the Isle of Wight which Sea Containers retained in 1990 but Stena's purchase of the company for £259 million severely stretched the Swedish company and amongst the

*The **Pride of Burgundy** was originally ordered for the Dover-Zeebrugge service but with additional capacity required on the Dover-Calais service she was later re-designed as a passenger ship.* (Miles Cowsill)

early casualties was the Folkestone - Boulogne link. While Townsend Thoresen and then P&O European Ferries were constructing new superferries and upgrading their service, Sealink Stena Line continued to run with converted and second hand vessels introducing the *Fantasia* in 1990 followed by the *Stena Invicta* with the ro-pax ferry *Stena Challenger* in 1991. After an £8 million refit the *Stena Empereur* (ex *Stena Jutlandica*) joined the Calais service in July 1996 after which the 'Challenger' sailed to the Holyhead station.

The Sealink and Stena operation at Dover was always run as a joint venture with French partners Sealink SNAT but this ceased at the end of 1995 when the French floated their own company known as SeaFrance. It is of interest that this is still marketed as 'Sealink' across the Channel.

Stena Line operated all three of its smaller fast craft at various times, the last to be used being the 74 metre *Stena Lynx* during winter 1997/98, and the *Stena Cambria* (formerly the *St. Anselm*) also provided extra tonnage after the Stena/SNCF split but the fleet was an odd mixture of vessels catering for a specific end of the market with their Stena Service Concept.

During July 1996 the Department of Trade and Industry gave both P&O European Ferries and Stena Line UK Ltd the 'amber' light allowing them to adopt some form of co-operation in response to the Channel Tunnel. A Memorandum of Understanding was signed that October when it was agreed that both companies would supply fourteen vessels (8 from P&OEF and 5 from Stena in addition to a fast craft) for the Dover - Zeebrugge, Dover - Calais and Newhaven - Dieppe routes. After further delays, Government permission for the 'Joint Venture' was given in November 1997 and the new company was officially launched on 9th March 1998. The vessels concerned were as follows:

Pride of Dover	renamed *P&OSL Dover*
Stena Empereur	renamed *P&OSL Provence*
Pride of Calais	renamed *P&OSL Calais*
Stena Fantasia	renamed *P&OSL Canterbury*
Pride of Burgundy	renamed *P&OSL Burgundy*
Stena Invicta	chartered and renamed *Color Viking*
Pride of Kent	renamed *P&OSL Kent*
Stena Cambria	sold February 1999
Pride of Bruges	renamed *P&OSL Picardy*.
	withdrawn February 2000
Stena Antrim	withdrawn March 1998
European Seaway	
European Pathway	
European Highway	
Elite (fast craft)	handed back to Stena October 1998

The original plan was for the *Pride of Bruges* to be switched to the

Newhaven - Dieppe service and trials were duly made. However, the *Stena Antrim* was withdrawn and sold and sister vessel *Stena Cambria*, with her more modern interior, was placed on the link to operate with the fast craft, *Elite* (formerly the *Stena Lynx III*). The 'Invicta' was immediately dispensed with, as with only one freight deck her use would be limited on the Calais link and so she never operated for the new company. The Dieppe link continued to lose money and the *Elite* was withdrawn from service as being unreliable and prone to delays or cancellations in bad weather. P&O Stena Line eventually closed the link on 31st January 1999 after which the French crews from the *Stena Cambria* were switched to the Zeebrugge freighter *European Pathway*. At the time, this vessel was enduring a prolonged period off service with a broken gear box and finding themselves a ship short for the Zeebrugge link duly chartered the *Stena Royal* which had been laid-up at

*The **P&OSL Canterbury** was converted from a freight vessel to a passenger ferry for the Dover-Calais route in 1989.* (FotoFlite)

Dunkerque since the closure of RMT's Ostend - Ramsgate link in February 1997. As the *Prins Filip*, the former flagship of the Belgian Government's fleet, this vessel represented that concern's last effort to save the ailing link. She was a splendid vessel which had entered service in 1992 and was built with the finest materials that the Belgian taxpayer could afford. One of Stena's numerous companies had purchased the idle vessel in June 1998 and this was her first service since the Ostend link had closed. Although much mechanical work was required, it was soon realised that the *Stena Royal* was too good a ship to lose and her charter was duly extended (with an option to purchase) at which time she was renamed *P&OSL Aquitaine*. After a major internal and mechanical refit, the ship took up sailings to Calais during November 1999.

*The **P&OSL Provence** was originally built for Stena Line's Frederikshavn-Gothenburg service. In 1997 she was transferred to the Dover-Calais route.* (FotoFlite)

P&OSL Calais leaving Calais for Dover in September 1999. (John Hendy)

John Hendy

Miles Cowsill

Gross tons	26,433
Net	11,399
Deadweight	4,203
Length (o.a.)	169.60m
Breadth (Extr.)	28.27m
Draught (max)	6.12m
Passenger capacity	2,290
Vehicles (max)	650 cars/100 x 15m freight units
Builders	Schichau-Unterweser AG, Bremen-Vegesack Germany
Yard No	93
Built	1987
Entered service with P&O	1987
Engines	3 Sulzer Diesels
Speed (knots)	22.0
Call sign	GJCR
Usual route	Dover-Calais
Former Name	*Pride of Dover*

Gross tons	26,433
Net	11,399
Deadweight	4,213
Length (o.a.)	169.60m
Breadth (Extr.)	28.27m
Draught (max)	6.12m
Passenger capacity	2,290
Vehicles (max)	650 cars/100 x 15m freight units
Builders	Schichau-Unterweser AG, Bremen-Vegesack Germany
Yard No	94
Built	1987
Entered service with P&O	1987
Engines	3 Sulzer Diesels
Speed (knots)	22.0
Call sign	GJLY
Usual route	Dover-Calais
Former Name	*Pride of Calais*

John Hendy

FotoFlite

Gross tons	20,446
Net	6,133
Deadweight	3,379
Length (o.a.)	163.40m
Breadth (Extr.)	26.18m
Draught (max)	5.54m
Passenger capacity	1,825
Vehicles (max)	460 cars/64 x 15m freight units
Builders	Schichau-Unterweser AG, Bremerhaven, Germany
Yard No	2279
Built	1980
Entered service with P&O	1980
Engines	3 Sulzer Diesels
Speed (knots)	20.0
Call sign	GBGR
Usual route	Dover-Calais
Former Names	*Pride of Kent, Spirit of Free Enterprise*

Gross tons	28,833
Net	11,853
Deadweight	4,250
Length (o.a.)	163.40m
Breadth (Extr.)	27.70m
Draught (max)	6.35m
Passenger capacity	1,200
Vehicles (max)	710 Cars/120 lorries
Builders	Boelwerf, Temse Belgium
Yard No	1534
Built	1992 (completed Oct. 91)
Entered service with P&OSL	1999
Engines	4 Sulzer Diesels
Speed (knots)	21.0
Call sign	MYBY8
Usual route	Dover-Calais
Former Names	*Stena Royal, Prins Filip*

John Hendy

John Hendy

Gross tons	28,138
Net	8,649
Deadweight	5,875
Length (o.a.)	179.70m
Breadth (Extr.)	28.30m
Draught (max)	6.27m
Passenger capacity	1,420
Vehicles (max)	600 cars/120 x 15m vehicles
Builders	Schichau Seebeckwerft AG, Bremerhaven, Germany
Yard No	1074
Built	1993
Entered service with P&O	1993
Engines	4 Sulzer Diesels ZA 40 S
Speed (knots)	21.0
Call sign	MQSQ9
Usual route	Dover-Calais
Former Name	*Pride of Burgundy*

Gross tons	25,122
Net	11,331
Deadweight	3,450
Length (o.a.)	163.51m
Breadth (Extr.)	27.64m
Draught (max)	6.52m
Passenger capacity	1,800
Vehicles (max)	650 cars/66 trailers
Builders	Kockums AB, Malmö, Sweden
Yard No	569
Built	1980
Entered service with P&OSL	1998
Engines	2 Sulzer Diesels
Speed (knots)	19.00
Call sign	MYHL3
Usual route	Dover-Calais
Former Names	*Stena Fantasia, Fantasia, Fiesta, Tzarevetz, Scandinavia*

P&OSL PROVENCE

John Hendy

Gross tons	28,559
Net	8,568
Deadweight	3,980
Length (o.a.)	156.20m
Breadth (Extr.)	28.46m
Draught (max)	6.32m
Passenger capacity	2,036
Vehicles (max)	550
Builders	CNM, Dunkerque, France
Yard No	310
Built	1983
Entered service with P&OSL	1998
Engines	4 CCM Sulzer Diesels
Speed (knots)	21.0
Call sign	MWYB4
Usual route	Dover-Calais
Former Names	*Stena Empereur, Stena Jutlandica*

EUROPEAN HIGHWAY

Miles Cowsill

Gross tons	22,986
Net	6,895
Deadweight	7,550
Length (o.a.)	179.70m
Breadth (Extr.)	28.30m
Draught (max)	6.27m
Passenger capacity	200
Vehicles (max)	124 x 15m freight units
Builders	Schichau Seebeckwerft AG, Bremerhaven Germany
Yard No	1073
Built	1992
Entered service with P&O	1992
Engines	4 Sulzer Diesels
Speed (knots)	21.0
Call sign	MQCJ2
Usual route	Dover-Zeebrugge

P&O Stena Line

P&O Stena Line

Gross tons	22,986
Net	6,895
Deadweight	7,509
Length (o.a.)	179.70m
Breadth (Extr.)	28.30m
Draught (max)	6.27m
Passenger capacity	200
Vehicles (max)	124 x 15m freight units
Builders	Schichau Seebeckwerft AG, Bremerhaven, Germany
Yard No	1076
Built	1991
Entered service with P&O	1992
Engines	4 Sulzer Diesels
Speed (knots)	21.0
Call sign	MPQZ6
Usual route	Dover-Zeebrugge

Gross tons	22,986
Net	6,895
Deadweight	7,432
Length (o.a.)	179.70m
Breadth (Extr.)	28.30m
Draught (max)	6.27m
Passenger capacity	200
Vehicles (max)	124 x 15m freight units
Builders	Schichau Seebeckwerft AG, Bremerhaven, Germany
Yard No	1075
Built	1991
Entered service with P&O	1991
Engines	4 Sulzer Diesels
Speed (knots)	21.0
Call sign	MPDG3
Usual route	Dover-Zeebrugge

P&O Portsmouth

The origins of P&O Portsmouth go back to 1964 when the entrepreneurial Norwegian businessman Otto Thoresen commenced a new and revolutionary ferry service linking Southampton and Cherbourg.

Thoresen had crossed the English Channel from time to time and was unimpressed by the services then operated by the British and French nationalised railway companies. His famous words, "You needn't be a genius to do better than this" were indeed prophetic and he observed that both England west of Dover and France west of Boulogne were without any roll on service at a time when the port of Southampton was looking for a new operator to fill the place in the Outer Dock vacated by the withdrawal of British Railways' service to the Channel Islands. Cherbourg too was experiencing problems with a slow decline in the trans-Atlantic passenger trade.

Pride of Bilbao. (Miles Cowsill)

fact that they were the most technically advanced ferries in operation in the English Channel all helped to thrust Thoresen Car Ferries to the forefront of the British ferry scene. Thoresen's philosophy that a ferry journey was to be enjoyed and not endured helped to cast away the doom and despondency of the British Railways era and taught them a lesson which they would never forget. After the first three weeks in operation, advance bookings showed that the Thoresen service would be a success.

A third 'Viking' was duly ordered after just two months of operation and entered service in June 1965. From the start Thoresen looked at route expansion. Winter service across the River Plate was investigated but prevented by an unstable political situation in Argentina. Plymouth - Spain was also mooted but instead off season charters were found for at least one

The *Viking I*'s keel was laid at Tonsberg on Oslo Fjord in October 1963 and she was delivered to her owners at the end of the following April ready to take up service on 11th May. She was soon followed by the *Viking II* and following a further withdrawal by British Railways, on 20th July a second link was opened to Le Havre.

The Thoresen ferries were an immediate success. With their drive-through decks (they were the first ferries in UK waters to be so built therefore allowing the carriage of mixed traffic, ie cars, passengers *and* lorries), bright orange hulls, clean Scandinavian lines and interiors and the

vessel while the other two continued with reduced crossings from Southampton. In June 1967, continued expansion saw the freight-only ro-ro vessel *Viking IV* take up service to Le Havre.

During July 1968, Thoresen Car Ferries was taken-over by George Nott Industries Ltd. of Coventry - the owners of Townsend Car Ferries at Dover. The merger provided a much stronger operations unit and provided considerable scope for improvements in operational efficiency. As far as the general public were concerned things remained the same as usual although after 1976, the Townsend fleet at Dover adopted the

Thoresen orange hull livery. The merger produced the European Ferries Group and during November the *Viking II* was transferred to the Dover - Zeebrugge link for six weeks while the *Free Enterprise II* became a regular addition to the summer Cherbourg sailings as from 1970.

Further expansion occurred when in December 1970, the EFG announced a five year expansion programme which included three Danish-built 'Super Viking' class ships for Southampton. The first vessel, *Viking Venturer,* entered service in January 1975 was to be followed by the *Viking Valiant* but instead of sailing immediately for the English Channel the company decided to introduce her on their new link between Felixstowe and Zeebrugge on which she commenced service during May. The third vessel was the *Viking Voyager* which arrived at Felixstowe in January 1976 thereby releasing the 'Valiant' for Southampton. A fourth ferry, the *Viking Viscount*, was later ordered.

The year 1976 was the beginning of the end as far as the ferry operations at Southampton were concerned. In that year nearby Portsmouth opened its doors to cross-Channel ro-ro traffic and in April the *Viking I* was renamed *Viking Victory* and switched to operate on a seasonal link with Cherbourg. The advantages of Portsmouth were plain to see with excellent port infrastructure, shorter crossing times to France and the absence of union problems which had so frequently plagued Southampton. Each year more and more sailings were transferred to Portsmouth until by the final day of 1983 only freight workings remained at Southampton as there was not enough storage space at Portsmouth. Twelve months later all Townsend Thoresen sailings were transferred.

With the new and larger vessels now in service, the original 'Vikings' were replaced. The first to be sold was the *Viking II* which became Sealink's *Earl William* in 1976. The workings of the *Viking III* became increasingly peripatetic as were those of the *Viking Victory* out-of-season. The freighter *Viking IV* was sold in 1981 to be followed in the next year by the *Viking III*. The 'Victory' completed service at the close of 1982 (being replaced by the

Otto Thoresen built two Viking vessels for his successful Southampton-Cherbourg/Le Havre services in 1964. The **Viking Victory** *(ex* **Viking I**) *is pictured here leaving Portsmouth during her first season on the Portsmouth-Cherbourg route.* (Miles Cowsill)

Free Enterprise V from Dover). The original 'Viking' was subsequently disposed of and much to the credit of Otto Thoresen remains in operation today.

The *Viking IV's* place in the fleet was taken by the former ASN vessel *Europic Ferry* but when she was requisitioned for the Falkland's War between April and July 1982, her one time running partner *Gaelic Ferry* was transferred from the Felixstowe - Rotterdam route.

A further period of dockers' unrest at Southampton saw the transfer of the two ship P&O Ferries Le Havre service to Portsmouth in December 1984 and in the following month P&O announced that they had sold their

*P&O Normandy Ferries opened a rival ferry service to that of Thoresen Car Ferries between Southampton and Le Havre in 1967. The British registered **Dragon** is seen arriving at Southampton.* (Miles Cowsill)

appropriate. Normandy Ferries had also commenced services to Lisbon, Tangier and Casablanca and ordered a large cruise ferry, the *Eagle,* to operate these new routes. Prior to her arrival the *Dragon* and *Leopard* maintained them with reduced passenger certificates but the service proved to be a failure and the *Eagle* was laid up for sale in October 1975. A further unsuccessful service using the *SF Panther* (ex *Peter Pan*) operated from Southampton to San Sebastian between November 1973 and November 1975.

The *Dragon* and *Leopard* continued although for marketing purposes the trading name 'Normandy Ferries' was dropped in favour of P&O Ferries early in 1980 at which time the ships received pale blue hulls.

The transfer of 'Super Vikings' 'Viscount' and 'Voyager' from the Felixstowe - Zeebrugge route to Portsmouth occurred in May 1987. At this time the *Leopard* was sold and the *Dragon* transferred to Cairnryan as the *Ionic Ferry*.

With continued need for freight space, the *Viking Venturer* and *Viking Valiant* were 'jumboized' during 1985-86 when their superstructures were lifted and a complete new lorry deck was inserted. This did nothing to improve their original design but enabled the twins to cope with the increased trade on the Le Havre link.

With the take-over of the European Ferries Group by the P&O Group in January 1987 and the birth of P&O European Ferries in the following October, the bright Thoresen livery disappeared in favour of the dark blue hulls and funnels of the new company. During 1989 - twenty five years since the commencement of the Thoresen service - the four ships were renamed with 'Pride' prefixes as follows:

Viking Venturer	Pride of Hampshire
Viking Valiant	Pride of Le Havre
Viking Voyager	Pride of Cherbourg
Viking Viscount	Pride of Winchester

The next major step in the development of P&O European Ferries at

Channel interests (both here and at Dover) to the European Ferries Group for £12.5 million. The P&O ship *Dragon* and the French-flagged *Leopard* continued on the Le Havre route while the 'Super Vikings' were switched to Cherbourg.

The company had commenced operations to Le Havre in June 1967. The ships had traded under the banner of Normandy Ferries - the *Dragon* being provided by Southern Ferries, a subsidiary of the General Steam Navigation Company, (a member of the P&O Group) - while the *Leopard* was French crewed and flagged and owned by the Societe Anonyme de Gerance et d' Armement (SAGA) and entered service in the following May. Crossings were also made between Le Havre and Rosslare between June 1968 and October 1971 after which time traffic across the Channel had grown to such an extent that the Irish diversion was no longer deemed

Portsmouth was the three year charter of the Swedish superferry *Olympia* in order to operate a new service linking Portsmouth with Bilbao in Spain. One of the largest ferries in the world, the ship was enormous with accommodation for up to 600 cars and 2,447 passengers on her 30 hour schedule. She was renamed *Pride of Bilbao* and entered service in April 1993.

Ever mindful of their now ageing fleet, P&O European Ferries looked for further charters to replace the former Felixstowe 'Super Vikings' which were by now too small for the traffic on offer. After an unsuccessful bid for two more Viking Line vessels from the Baltic Sea sphere of operation, in March 1994 the company secured the five year charter of the twin five year old Olau Line ships which had experienced major manning problems with their German unions on the southern North Sea crossing linking Sheerness with Vlissingen. The spacious cruise-ferries boasted excellent and spacious accommodation and were regular winners of the AA's prestigious Five Star awards. Their popular service finally closed in May after which the *Olau Britannia* was renamed *Pride of Portsmouth* and the *Olau Hollandia* became the *Pride of Le Havre*. The previous ship of that name was renamed *Pride of Cherbourg* whilst the original *Pride of Cherbourg* received the suffix 'II' for the brief remainder of her service.

The new ships were destined for the Le Havre link whilst the stretched 'Super Vikings' found a new home on the Cherbourg route. The *Pride of Winchester* and *Pride of Cherbourg II* were both sold for further trading that summer and remain in service for their respective owners in Greece and in the Canary Islands.

With the Portsmouth-based fleet now reconstituted, the company must now look towards the eventual replacement of the original pair of 'Super Vikings.' In a bid to improve their popular Cherbourg link, in May 1998 they chartered the very successful Austal Ships 82 metre catamaran *SuperStar Express* from Malaysian owners. She carries up to 800 passengers and 175 cars across the Channel in just 2 hours 45 minutes. So popular

*During the early seventies Townsend Thoresen ordered four 'Super Viking' vessels for their Southampton and Felixstowe operations. The **Pride of Cherbourg** (ex **Viking Voyager**) was originally built for the Felixstowe operation but later transferred to Portsmouth services. (FotoFlite)*

was the new fast ferry operation that a larger craft was introduced on the Portsmouth-Cherbourg route in April 2000. The new vessel *Portsmouth Express* offered increased capacity for cars, which the company had been seeking, and the *SuperStar Express* was transferred to the Irish Sea in place of the *Jetliner*.

*The **Pride of Bilbao** (ex. Olympia) makes an impressive sight as she arrives at Portsmouth from Bilbao in August 1998. (Miles Cowsill)*

P&O Portsmouth

FotoFlite

Gross tons	5,902
Net	2,441
Deadweight	450
Length (o.a.)	91.30m
Breadth (Extr.)	26.00m
Draught (max)	3.70m
Passenger capacity	868
Vehicles (max)	225
Builders	InCat, Australia
Yard No	47
Built	1998
Entered service with P&O	2000
Engines	4 Caterpillar Diesels
Speed (knots)	41.0
Call sign	C6FM4
Usual route	Portsmouth-Cherbourg
Former Name	*Catalonia, Catalonia L*

Gross tons	37,583
Net	23,730
Deadweight	4,300
Length (o.a.)	176.82m
Breadth (Extr.)	28.40m
Draught (max)	6.71m
Passenger capacity	2,563
Vehicles (max)	600 cars/62 x 15m freight units
Builders	Wartsila, Turku, Finland
Yard No	1290
Built	1986
Entered service with P&O	1993
Engines	4 Wartsila Pielstick Diesels
Speed (knots)	22.0
Call sign	MTDM5
Usual route	Portsmouth-Bilbao/Cherbourg
Former Name	*Olympia*

Miles Cowsill

Miles Cowsill

Gross tons	33,336
Net	17,001
Deadweight	4,100
Length (o.a.)	161.00m
Breadth (Extr.)	29.60m
Draught (max)	6.52m
Passenger capacity	1,600
Vehicles (max)	575 cars/89 x 15m freight units
Builders	Schichau Seebeckwerft AG, Bremerhaven Germany
Yard No	1068
Built	1990
Entered service with P&O	1994
Engines	4 Sulzer Diesels
Speed (knots)	21.0
Call sign	MSTK8
Usual route	Portsmouth-Le Havre
Former Name	*Olau Britannia*

Gross tons	33,336
Net	17,001
Deadweight	4,100
Length (o.a.)	161.00m
Breadth (Extr.)	29.60m
Draught (max)	6.52m
Passenger capacity	1,600
Vehicles (max)	575 cars/89 x 15m freight vehicles
Builders	Schichau Seebeckwerft AG, Bremerhaven, Germany
Yard No	1067
Built	1989
Entered service with P&O	1994
Engines	4 Sulzer Diesels
Speed (knots)	21.0
Call sign	MSTJ8
Usual route	Portsmouth-Le Havre
Former Name	*Olau Hollandia*

Miles Cowsill

Miles Cowsill

Gross tons	14,760
Net	4,782
Deadweight	2,194
Length (o.a.)	143.66m
Breadth (Extr.)	23.47m
Draught (max)	5.40m
Passenger capacity	920
Vehicles (max)	380 cars/53 x 15m freight units
Builders	Aalborg Vaerft A/S. Aalborg, Denmark
Yard No 1068	204
Built	1975
Entered service with P&O	1975
Engines	3 Stork-Werkspoor Diesels
Speed (knots)	18.0
Call sign	GURE
Usual route	Portsmouth-Cherbourg
Former Names	*Pride of Le Havre, Viking Valiant*

Gross tons	14,760
Net	4,782
Deadweight	2,192
Length (o.a.)	143.66m
Breadth (Extr.)	23.47m
Draught (max)	5.40m
Passenger capacity	920
Vehicles (max)	380 cars/53 x 15m freight units
Builders	Aalborg Vaerft A/S, Aalborg, Denmark
Yard No 1068	203
Built	1975
Entered service with P&O	1975
Engines	3 Stork-Werkspoor Diesels
Speed (knots)	18.0
Call sign	GUPM
Usual route	Portsmouth-Cherbourg
Former Name	*Viking Venturer*

CHAPTER 8

P&O Irish Sea

P&O European Ferries (Irish Sea) was formed in 1998 by the merger of the Cairnryan-based service of P&O European Ferries (Felixstowe) Ltd. and Pandoro Ltd. who operated the routes from Ardrossan - Larne, Fleetwood - Larne, Liverpool - Dublin and Rosslare - Cherbourg.

The Atlantic Steam Navigation Company commenced operations with the chartered tank landing craft *Empire Cedric* between the Lancashire port of Preston and Larne in May 1948. Her success saw the further charters of the *Empire Doric, Empire Gaelic* and *Empire Cymric* and the opening of a second link to Belfast by the 'Gaelic' in 1950.

During 1956 the entire fleet of LSTs (Landing Ship (Tank)) was requisitioned by the Government during the Suez Crisis and chartered German ships were hastily introduced to keep the services going while in the following year the company acquired their first purpose-built ships. A product of the Wm. Denny & Bros. yard at Dumbarton the *Bardic Ferry* and *Ionic Ferry* were the world's first commercial roll on - roll off vessels and carried not just lorries but had sufficient headroom on their vehicle decks to accommodate a double decker bus. Government requirements meant that the vehicle decks were strengthened to carry tanks in case of future emergencies and up to twenty containers could be carried on their upper decks. First and Second Class accommodation for 55 passengers was provided, each with their own dining rooms and lounges.

European Leader. (Gordon Hislip)

The *Bardic Ferry* made her maiden voyage between Preston and Larne in September 1957 while the 'Ionic' entered service on the same link in October 1958 at which time the premier ship was transferred to the Tilbury - Antwerp route. Two further larger vessels of this type were duly ordered from the Ailsa shipyard at Troon and the *Cerdic Ferry* (Rotterdam service) and *Doric Ferry* (Antwerp service) entered service at Tilbury in November 1961 and April 1962 by which time the 'Bardic' was back on the Irish Sea.

With the new vessels in operation, the LST fleet was gradually reduced until the final such ship, the *Empire Nordic,* was withdrawn in December 1966. With no relief ship during the annual overhauls, ASN chartered Thoresen's *Viking I* to serve the Preston - Larne route during January 1967.

During the 1960s, ASN had purchased a small pier at Cairnryan on Loch Ryan, Wigtownshire, for £60,000 and in 1970 they decided to upgrade it for a new short-sea service. The European Ferries Group (EFG) acquired the ASN for £5.5 million in November 1971 and immediately injected new ideas, new ships and a new style of service. The closure of Preston, with its tidal problems and a long and narrow course up the River Ribble, occurred in March 1973 and the following day the *Ionic Ferry* (with an increased passenger certificate for 219) sailed to Cairnryan for trials before commencing the new service across the North Channel in July. The closure of Preston - Larne saw the Belfast services doubled using the *Bardic Ferry* and *Doric Ferry* but at the close of July 1974 the passage was terminated and all traffic was in future shipped through Cairnryan which had by this time gained a second linkspan. October 1973 had seen the EFG purchase the Larne Harbour Company.

In an effort to boost seasonal traffic on the crossing, the Dover ferry *Free Enterprise III* was introduced on the Cairnryan - Larne route between July - October 1974. She then returned south at which time the *Bardic Ferry* took up station. The small, stern loader *Free Enterprise I* was transferred to the link for the 1975 season after which the *Free Enterprise IV* appeared in 1976 and was such a success that she remained for the next ten years. The year 1976 also saw the sale of the 'Bardic' and the 'Ionic' to Greek owners.

The ro-ro vessel *European Gateway*, which had entered service at Felixstowe during June 1975, was also transferred to the North Channel link in March 1980 to cover for the annual overhaul of the 'FE IV' and the *Doric Ferry* while that winter she was sent to Amsterdam to be lengthened and to increase her passenger capacity to 326 before operating the North Channel service on a permanent basis with the 'FE IV'. Now spare vessels, in the following year the 'Doric' and 'Cerdic' were offered for sale. Sadly the 'Gateway' was lost off Felixstowe during a period in which she was covering for overhaul in December 1981. The *Gaelic Ferry* was then transferred to the Ulster link until replaced by the *Europic Ferry* in March 1983.

Further fleet reshuffles saw the *Free Enterprise IV* return to Dover in July 1986 while her place was taken by the former Southampton-based *Dragon* which was renamed *Ionic Ferry*. The 'Europic' and 'Ionic' partnership lasted until 1992 when the stretched Dover - Zeebrugge twins *Pride of Sandwich* (ex *Free Enterprise VI*) and *Pride of Walmer* (ex *Free Enterprise VII*) were replaced in the Dover Strait and made available for the North Channel becoming the *Pride of Ailsa* and *Pride of Rathlin*. Capacity was certainly boosted on the shortest route to Ireland and the last ASN ship, the *Europic Ferry*, was downgraded to freight-only purposes and was renamed *European*

*The former ASN vessel **Gaelic Ferry** is seen here in her Townsend Thoresen livery whilst operating between Felixstowe and Europoort. (FotoFlite)*

Freighter. The 'Ionic' was withdrawn and sold to Greek owners.

In June 1996, P&O European Ferries chartered the revolutionary £20 million monohull fast craft, *Jetliner*. The 600 passenger, 160 car vessel crosses the North Channel in just one hour and offers six sailings each day. Her arrival saw the withdrawal of the *Pride of Ailsa* which was sold to Egypt while former Dover ro-ro vessels *European Endeavour* and *European Trader* joined the route to boost freight capacity in September 1995 and February 1996. In April 2000 the *Jetliner* was replaced by the *Superstar Express*.

The remaining 'Free Enterprise' class vessel, the *Pride of Rathlin* is due to be withdrawn from service in June 2000 after the delivery of the *European Causeway*, a 23 knot new ro-pax ferry which is presently being built in Japan. The new ship will reduce conventional crossing times to just 105

The Puma (now European Seafarer) leaves Larne for Fleetwood on Pandoro's daily freight service between Northern Ireland and England. (Miles Cowsill)

minutes and will accommodate 375 cars (or 107 commercial vehicles) and 410 passengers.

The Pandoro part of P&O European Ferries (Irish Sea) can trace its history back to 1974. The name is a clever acronym of P AND O RO (ie roll on). Seeking to increase its road haulage and freight interests, P&O had purchased the well-established Coast Lines (who were at this time 25% share holders in North Sea Ferries) in 1971 and at the same time the Group reorganised its 120 subsidiaries which were absorbed into five new divisions.

Long established names such as Coast Lines, its subsidiary the Belfast Steamship Company (operating the overnight Liverpool - Belfast link with the new car ferries *Ulster Prince* and *Ulster Queen*) and Burns & Laird (operators of the *Lion* on the daylight Ardrossan - Belfast route) disappeared and the operating title of P&O Ferries (Irish Sea Services) was adopted.

In 1972 the formation of Ferrymasters (Ireland) Ltd. (the parent company of which Coast Lines owned an interest) soon saw a new service operating between Fleetwood and Larne which commenced operation in June 1973. In the following November the British Transport Docks Board started work on a ro-ro terminal at the Lancashire port and in 1974 P&O purchased the new ro-ro vessels *Bison* and *Buffalo* from Stena Line for £8 million. A further £1.25 million was invested in ro-ro units to be used in connection with the new ships.

Then in December 1974 they founded Pandoro providing a local transport operation for shippers to Ireland into which Ferrymasters (Ireland) was absorbed. In addition to the new service to Larne, one of the ships also served Dublin in a new joint venture with the British & Irish Steam Packet Co. (B+I). The *Bison* was first in service in February 1975, actually operating her maiden voyage from the Royal Seaforth Dock in Liverpool, while the *Buffalo* followed in March.

The ro-ro trade expanded rapidly at a time when the 'troubles' in Northern Ireland were having a profound effect on the tourist and passenger/ car market. Smaller, less profitable services were soon axed as the new Pandoro services went from strength to strength and services to and from from Garston, Preston, Warrenpoint, Newry and Londonderry were all closed.

P&O unveiled their 'new image' in October 1975 when the Belfast Steamship Co. and Burns & Laird Lines became P&O Ferries (Irish Sea Services) and the *Ulster Queen* and *Ulster Prince* were duly painted in their pale blue livery.

The *Lion* was withdrawn from service at Ardrossan in February 1976 after which she was sent to the Dover Strait to commence a new Normandy Ferries link with Boulogne. The long-established overnight Liverpool -

*The **European Leader** currently operates the Liverpool-Dublin service of P&O Irish Sea. She is due to be replaced on the route by new tonnage in 2001.* (Miles Cowsill)

Belfast route was finally withdrawn in November 1981 with losses estimated at £1 million after which the "Ulster" boats were laid-up pending sale in Ostend.

Meanwhile at Liverpool, Pandoro built a ramp and terminal at the North West Alexandra Dock and chartered then purchased the four year old *Union Melbourne* which, after stretching, eventually became the *Puma*. This proved so successful that the *Bison* and the *Buffalo* received similar extensions in 1981 and 1988. Further increases in freight saw the *Bison* receive an extra deck in 1995 while three years later the *Buffalo* was given hers.

Further large ro-ro vessels to join Pandoro have been the *Ibex* which was built in 1979 after which she was chartered to North Sea Ferries

between 1980 and 1995 during which time she was named firstly *Norsea* and then *Norsky* before returning to the Liverpool - Dublin service under her original name. She too received an extra deck in 1996.

The *Viking Trader* was built for Stena Line in 1977 but was taken on charter by P&O European Ferries (Portsmouth) Ltd. in 1983 at which time she adopted a familiar 'Viking ' name. She was transferred to Pandoro in 1989 and eventually renamed the *Leopard* for the Fleetwood - Dublin route.

In 1993, Pandoro inaugurated a new service linking Rosslare with Cherbourg and acquired the former Dover - Zeebrugge freighter *European Clearway* in order to operate the link. Replaced at Dover by new tonnage, the 'Clearway' had been transferred to Portsmouth - Le Havre in 1992 before her 'sale' to P&O Group partners. In January 1996 the vessel was renamed *Panther*. The Ardrossan - Larne link received the services of the 1978-built *Merchant Valiant* in 1993. Two years later she was purchased and renamed the *Lion*.

During late 1997 and early 1998, in preparation of the formation of P&O European Ferries (Irish Sea), the entire Pandoro fleet was renamed thus:

> *Bison* became *European Pioneer*
> *Buffalo* became *European Leader*
> *Ibex* became *European Envoy*
> *Leopard* became *European Navigator*
> *Lion* became *European Highlander*
> *Panther* became *European Pathfinder*
> *Puma* became *European Seafarer*.

New tonnage was announced in 1999 when a £33 million ro-pax was ordered from Mitsubishi of Japan for the Liverpool - Dublin route for delivery early in 2001. The vessel will see the transfer of the *European Leader* to the Fleetwood station and further orders of this type could well be forthcoming as the company try to expand the passenger/ tourist car market on the Dublin route and earlier vessels become due for replacement.

P&O Irish Sea

William Mayes

Gross tons	20,800
Net	-
Deadweight	4,335
Length (o.a.)	156.20m
Breadth (Extr.)	23.40m
Draught (max)	5.50m
Passenger capacity	410
Vehicles (max)	375 or 107 x 13.5 freight units
Builders	Mitsubishi Heavy Industries, Shimonoeki, Japan
Yard No	1065
Built	2000
Entered service with P&O	Due August 2000
Engines	4 Wertsila diesels
Speed (knots)	23.0
Call sign	Applied for
Usual route	Larne-Cairnryan

Gross tons	5,517
Net	1,656
Deadweight	340
Length (o.a.)	82.30m
Breadth (Extr.)	23.30m
Draught (max)	2.81m
Passenger capacity	800
Vehicles (max)	175
Builders	Austal Ships, Fremantle, Australia
Yard No	60
Built	1997
Entered service with P&O	1998
Engines	4 MTU Diesels
Speed (knots)	38.5
Call sign	3FFX9
Usual route	Larne-Cairnryan (As from April 2000)
Former Name	*SuperStar Express Langkawi*

Miles Cowsill

FotoFlite

Gross tons	12,503
Net	3,750
Deadweight	2,136
Length (o.a.)	139.40m
Breadth (Extr.)	22.44m
Draught (max)	4.75m
Passenger capacity	610
Vehicles (max)	340 cars/60 x 12m freight units
Builders	IHC Holland,/Werf Gusto Yard,Schiedam, Rotterdam, Holland
Yard No	882
Built	1973
Entered service with P&O	1973
Engines	3 Stork-Werkspoor Diesels
Speed (knots)	17.0
Call sign	ZCBO8
Usual route	Larne-Cairnryan
Former Names	*Pride of Walmer, Free Enterprise VII*

Gross tons	8,097
Net	2,429
Deadweight	3,767
Length (o.a.)	117.85m
Breadth (Extr.)	20.30m
Draught (max)	5.09m
Passenger capacity	107
Vehicles (max)	76 x 15m freight units
Builders	Schichau Unterweser AG, Bremerhaven, Germany
Yard No	2275
Built	1978
Entered service with P&O	1978
Engines	2 Stork-Werkspoor Diesels
Speed (knots)	18.4
Call sign	ZCBN6
Usual route	Larne-Cairnryan
Former Name	*European Enterprise*

FotoFlite

Gordon Hislip

Gross tons	8,007		Gross tons	5,897
Net	2,402		Net	1,769
Deadweight	3,593		Deadweight	3,046
Length (o.a.)	117.91m		Length (o.a.)	116.30m
Breadth (Extr.)	20.30m		Breadth (Extr.)	18.22m
Draught (max)	5.03m		Draught (max)	5.36m
Passenger capacity	132		Passenger capacity	12
Vehicles (max)	76 x 15m freight units		Vehicles (max)	71x15m freight units
Builders	Schichau Unterweser AG, Bremerhaven, Germany		Builders	Rickmers Rhederei, Bremerhaven, Germany
Yard No 1068	2258		Yard No	390
Built	1975		Built	1978
Entered service with P&O	1975		Entered service with P&O	1995
Engines	2 Stork-Werkspoor Diesels		Engines	2 MaK Mashinenbau Diesels
Speed (knots)	17.5		Speed (knots)	15.5
Call sign	ZCBO		Call sign	C6HL7
Usual route	Larne-Cairnryan		Usual route	Larne-Adrossan(Troon 2001)
			Former Names	*Lion, Merchant Valiant, Salahala*

P&O

Gordon Hislip

Gross tons	14,387	Gross tons	12,879
Net	4,316	Net	3,864
Deadweight	4,385	Deadweight	4,377
Length (o.a.)	140.10m	Length (o.a.)	156.50m
Breadth (Extr.)	23.15m	Breadth (Extr.)	19.42m
Draught (max)	4.67m	Draught (max)	4.26m
Passenger capacity	60	Passenger capacity	80
Vehicles (max)	110	Vehicles (max)	90
Builders	J.J.Sietas KG, Schiffswerft GmbH, Hamburg, Germany	Builders	J.J.Sietas KG, Schiffswerft GmbH, Hamburg, Germany
Yard No	755	Yard No	756
Built	1975	Built	1975
Entered service with P&O	1975	Entered service with P&O	1975
Engines	2 Deutz Diesels	Engines	2 Deutz Diesels
Speed (knots)	18.5	Speed (knots)	18.5
Call sign	ZCBJ8	Call sign	ZCBF8
Usual route	Fleetwood-Larne	Usual route	Liverpool-Dublin
Former Name	*Bison*	Former Name	*Buffalo*

Gordon Hislip

Gordon Hislip

Gross tons	18,653
Net	5,595
Deadweight	4,267
Length (o.a.)	150.02m
Breadth (Extr.)	24.43m
Draught (max)	5.12m
Passenger capacity	70
Vehicles (max)	120
Builders	Mitsui Eng & SB. Co, Tamano, Japan
Yard No	1163
Built	1979
Entered service with P&O	1979
Engines	2 Mitsui Diesels
Speed (knots)	19.4
Call sign	ZCBB2
Usual route	Liverpool-Dublin
Former Names	*Ibex, Norsky, Norsea*

Gross tons	9,085
Net	2,726
Deadweight	3,775
Length (o.a.)	137.30m
Breadth (Extr.)	18.14m
Draught (max)	5.66m
Passenger capacity	48
Vehicles (max)	70
Builders	Osterreichische Schiffswerften AG, Korneuburg, Austria
Yard No	709
Built	1977
Entered service with P&O	1989
Engines	2 Deutz Diesels
Speed (knots)	16.0
Call sign	ZCBG3
Usual route	Larne-Cairnryan
Former Names	*Leopard, Viking Trader, Oster Bay, Manuare VII, Caribbean Sky, Federal Nova, Goya, Stena Trader*

Gordon Hislip

Gordon Hislip

Gross tons	10,957
Net	3,287
Deadweight	4,035
Length (o.a.)	141.81m
Breadth (Extr.)	19.41m
Draught (max)	5.80m
Passenger capacity	40
Vehicles (max)	93
Builders	J.J. Sietas KG Schiffswerft GmbH, Hamburg, Germany
Yard No	757
Built	1975
Entered service with P&O	1980
Engines	2 Deutz Diesels
Speed (knots)	18.0
Call sign	ZCAZ2
Usual route	Fleetwood-Larne
Former Names	*Puma, Union Trader, Union Melbourne*

Gross tons	8,023
Net	2,406
Deadweight	3,927
Length (o.a.)	117.85m
Breadth (Extr.)	20.27m
Draught (max)	5.03m
Passenger capacity	53
Vehicles (max)	76 x15m freight units
Builders	Schichau Unterweser AG, Bremerhaven, Germany
Yard No	2263
Built	1976
Entered service with P&O	1976
Engines	2 Stork-Werkspoor Diesels
Speed (knots)	18.4
Call sign	ZCAW5
Usual route	Rosslare-Cherbourg
Former Names	*Panther, European Clearway*

Gordon Hislip

P&O

Gross tons	11,086/7,606
Net	3,326/2,282
Deadweight	4,500/5,758
Length (o.a.)	136.00/122.32m
Breadth (Extr.)	20.50/19.80m
Draught (max)	7.70/6.20m
Passengers	12/12
Vehicles (max)	86 lorries/88 trailers
Builders	Kanda Zosencho K.K.,Kawajiri, Japan/
	Ast de Huelva, Huelva, Spain
Yard Nos.	337/570
Built	1991/1998
Entered service with P&O	1999/2000
Engines	2 Pielstick Diesels/2 Wartsila Diesels
Speed (knots)	20.8/17.0
Call signs	JM6038/ESFO
Usual route	Liverpool-Dublin
Former Names	*Loon-Plage, Kosie Maru, Iolaos/Dart 7, Lembitu*

Gross tons	24,500
Net	-
Deadweight	5,000
Length (o.a.)	170.00m
Breadth (Extr.)	24.00m
Draught (max)	6.00m
Passengers	405
Vehicles (max)	375 cars or 123 x 13.5m freight units
Builders	Mitsubishi Heavy Industries, Shimonoeki,
	Japan
Yard No	-
Built	2000
Entered service with P&O	Due January 2001
Engines	-
Speed (knots)	25.0
Call sign	Applied for
Usual route	Liverpool/Dublin as from 2001

CHAPTER 9

P&O North Sea Ferries

P&O North Sea Ferries was incorporated on New Year's Day 1997 after the Dutch Royal Nedlloyd Group had sold its 50% stake in North Sea Ferries to operating partners P&O. At the same time P&O European Ferries (Felixstowe) Ltd. was reorganised and that concern's Felixstowe-based operations were added to those of the new company.

The North Sea Ferries story was the brainchild of Mr. Ian Churcher who from an early time saw the changing trends in ferry traffic across the English Channel and anticipated that the movement of passengers, cars and freight by roll on - roll off vessel would eventually extend to the North Sea. In founding a company, he initially formed a consortium of six British, Dutch and German interests to invest in the new service.

During the mid-sixties, the British Rail subsidiary Associated Humber Line was operating the Hull (Riverside Quay) - Rotterdam (Parkhaven) service with the container vessels *Bolton Abbey* and *Melrose Abbey*. The twins had been built at Lowestoft in 1958/59 and latterly carried 88 passengers as well as crane loaded cars. During 1967/68 they were lengthened and new termini were duly required on both sides, Hull switching to the Alexandra Dock while the Rotterdam berth was moved out to Beatrixhaven.

North Sea Ferries sought to provide a daily overnight service in each direction from Hull's King George V Dock to Europoort at the mouth of Rotterdam's New Waterway. The *Norwave* (British crewed and flagged)

European Freeway and Norsea. (John May)

entered service in mid-December 1965 to be followed by the identical *Norwind* (Dutch crewed and flagged) in the following March. These comfortable ships provided accommodation for 249 passengers, 47 x 12 metre units and 70 cars and proved to be an immediate success. Quite simply the new company had given an increasingly mobile public and the freight industry what they wanted and the rival service was soon to feel the pinch of competition before being forced to close in November 1971.

As is often the case, new ships operating a new-style service soon become victims of their own success and this was certainly the case with the *Norwave* and *Norwind*. With North Sea Ferries firmly established the larger *Norland* (British) and *Norstar* (Dutch) duly entered service in June and December 1974. Boasting a passenger capacity for as many as 1,243 and space on their vehicle decks for 500 cars or 134 x 12 metre units, the arrival of the new ships saw the earlier pair transferred to a completely new link with the Belgian port of Zeebrugge. The port's original NSF terminal was through the locks in the Prins Filipdok but in May 1985 matters were greatly improved when the present terminal on the Leopold II Dam was opened.

With freight continuing to grow, during March 1977 North Sea Ferries opened a new link between Ipswich and Europoort which continued until April 1995.

The Falklands conflict saw the *Norland* requisitioned by the Ministry of Defence between April 1982 and February 1983 and being a ship short, NSF were forced to charter outside tonnage in order to keep their service operational. In the short term Sally Line's *Viking 6* was used until the larger Irish Continental Line's *Saint Patrick II* could be acquired. Following the victorious return of the battle-scarred *Norland*, plans were drawn up to stretch both 1974 twins by some 20 metres during which time their cargo capacity would be increased by 30%. The work was completed during summer 1987.

The £90 million third generation of North Sea Ferries were the magnificent *Norsea* (British) and *Norsun* (Dutch). The former was built at Govan Shipbuilders and entered service in May 1987 while the *Norsun* was built in Japan and joined the route four days later. Passenger capacity was provided for 1,250 but vehicle spaces had grown to accommodate as many

The Viking Voyager and Viking Viscount were the mainstay of the Felixstowe-Zeebrugge passenger service from 1975 to 1985 when both vessels were transferred to the Portsmouth operation. (FotoFlite)

as 850 cars or 180 x 12 metre units. They were the largest ships that could enter the King George Dock and leave just 1 ft. each side when they lock in or out of the basin. On the entry into service of the twin superferries, the *Norland* and *Norstar* returned to Germany to be lengthened before replacing the original twins on the Zeebrugge link. These were duly sold to Greek owners but were both victims of 'internal explosions' in mysterious circumstances whilst undergoing overhauls in 1988 and 1993.

On a happier note, new freight services linking Middlesbrough with Zeebrugge and Europoort were opened in May 1988 and March 1995.

Discussions for future generations of ferries had been underway for many years and it was appreciated from an early time that larger ships would require a riverside berth in the Humber. Accordingly in 1992 a pair of fast 'superfreighters' were ordered while work on an £11 million river terminal duly commenced. The Dutch-flagged *Norbank* entered service in

The Gaelic Ferry pictured on passage to Felixstowe in her original ASN colours. (FotoFlite)

*Following the transfer of the 'Super Viking' vessels to Portsmouth, the converted freight vessels **Pride of Suffolk** (pictured here) and **Pride of Flanders** maintained the Felixstowe-Zeebrugge passenger service. (FotoFlite)*

Ferry Service. The company was led by Lt. Col. Frank Bustard who had observed the potential of roll on - roll off during the last war and was determined to use former tank landing craft to operate his own civilian services. The company commenced operations from Tilbury - Hamburg and Preston - Larne in September 1946 and in May 1948 respectively but in April 1954 it was taken over by the British Transport Commission.

The North Sea links were transferred to the Felixstowe - Rotterdam (Europoort) service in July 1965 using the *Gaelic Ferry* (28 drivers and 65 lorries) of 1963. The nine hour crossing was a great improvement on the sixteen hours required on the Tilbury route and allowed greater flexibility and improved running costs. The excellent *Europic Ferry* joined the Europoort service in January 1968 and in September 1968 all ASN links were switched to the Suffolk port.

In 1971 the ASN was de-nationalised and sold to the European Ferries Group for £5.5 million. The deal involved eight vessels and with the acquisition of the Felixstowe Dock & Railway Company, the new parent company set out to develop the site into one of the world's largest container ports.

A passenger service to Zeebrugge was introduced by Thoresen's *Viking II* in October 1974 and she was joined by the new *Viking Valiant* in the following May. The arrival of sister ship *Viking Voyager* in January 1976 allowed the 'Valiant' to sail to the English Channel while the fourth of the series, *Viking Viscount*, joined the Zeebrugge link that May. A notable failure was the company's attempt to open a Felixstowe - Rotterdam passenger route using Thoresen's *Viking III*. The seven hour crossing commenced in March 1978 and was taken over by the *Viking Victory* in October while the *Viking III* was tried on an experimental Leith - Kristiansand link. Neither were repeated.

The year 1981 saw the EFG charter twin ro-ro vessels from Stena Line of Gothenburg. They were later renamed - in the ASN tradition of names ending in the letters 'ic' - *Baltic Ferry* and *Nordic Ferry* and provided much

October 1993 to be followed by the British *Norbay* in the following February.

In September 1996 North Sea Ferries announced that the P&O Group had purchased the 50% share of their partners Royal Nedlloyd for £25.5 million and that with effect from the New Year 1997, both North Sea Ferries and P&O European Ferries (Felixstowe) Ltd. would trade as P&O North Sea Ferries. During the following months all ships were repainted in the standard P&O ferry livery to reflect the change of ownership.

The Felixstowe-based operations were originally the preserve of the Atlantic Steam Navigation Company (ASN) who traded as the Transport

The Dutch registered Norstar *leaves the inner dock at Hull on her nightly service to Zeebrugge.* (Miles Cowsill)

extra capacity on the Europoort link before both being requisitioned by the Ministry of Defence during the Falklands War.

During a major reallocation of fleet in 1987, it was decided that the large multi-purpose 'Super Viking' Zeebrugge ships should be transferred to the Portsmouth - Cherbourg route. In a £5 million refit, the *Baltic Ferry* and the *Nordic Ferry* were to receive accommodation modules for 650 passengers to allow them to work the Zeebrugge link where they would also provide 30% extra freight space. Two more of the same class of South Korean-built ro-ro vessels were now chartered in the form of the *Hellas* (renamed *Doric Ferry*) and *Syria* (renamed *Cerdic Ferry*) which duly took up

the Europoort freight-only services in place of the earlier vessels. They were eventually purchased in 1994.

As with the Dover and Portsmouth fleets, the Felixstowe ships were also renamed during 1992 as follows:

Baltic Ferry became *Pride of Suffolk*
Nordic Ferry became *Pride of Flanders*
Cerdic Ferry became *European Freeway*
Doric Ferry became *European Tideway*

Even though it had been re-marketed as the Clipper Line in 1994, the closure of the Zeebrugge route to passengers in October 1995 was attributed to the run-down of the British army in Germany. Both ships had their accommodation modules removed but retained the names 'Suffolk' and 'Flanders' after being switched to run with their sisters on the Europoort link. Chartered tonnage was acquired to keep the Zeebrugge freight link operational.

With services from Middlesbrough (including P&O Trans European's route to Gothenburg), Hull and Felixstowe now under one management, P&O North Sea Ferries is a major force in the North Sea sphere of operations. The Middlesbrough - Zeebrugge freight route was greatly strengthened in July and November 1999 with the advent of the new *Norsky* and *Norstream* which allowed the smaller *Norking* and *Norqueen* to be switched to the Europoort service.

*In 1993 the **Norbay** (pictured here) and the **Norbank** were introduced on a new freight service between Hull and Europoort.* (Miles Cowsill)

*During 2001 the **Pride of Hull** and **Pride of Rotterdam** are due to enter service. This view shows the keel being laid to the first of the vessels at Fincantieri's yard in Venice .* (P&O North Sea Ferries)

The whole operation will be strengthened in 2001 with the introduction of the fourth generation of ferries on the Hull - Europoort route. Costing approximately £90 million each and named *Pride of Hull* and *Pride of Rotterdam*, the Italian-built vessels are programmed for delivery in April and December 2001. Each will have a gross tonnage of about 60,600 and will offer accommodation for 1,360 passengers, and 3,400 lane metres on three freight decks in addition to 1,500 metres of double-stacked container units and a special side-loading deck capable of carrying 250 cars.

Not only will these massive ferries replace the *Norsea* and *Norsun* but also the 'Super freighters' *Norbank* and *Norbay*. The former pair will move to the Hull - Zeebrugge route, replacing the *Norland* and *Norstar* which may be sold, while the freighters will transfer to the Felixstowe - Europoort link replacing the 'Flanders' and the 'Suffolk.'

British registered Norsea was built at Govan Shipbuilders, Glasgow. Her sister the Norsun was built in Japan. Both vessels are due to be transferred to the Hull-Zeebrugge service during the latter part of 2001. This picture shows the Norsea in her original livery leaving Hull. (Miles Cowsill)

P&O North Sea

John May

Gross tons	31,598
Net	18,174
Deadweight	6,403
Length (o.a.)	179.35m
Breadth (Extr.)	25.35m
Draught (max)	6.18m
Passenger capacity	1,250
Vehicles (max)	850 cars/ 180 Trailers
Builders	Nippon Kokan K.K., Japan
Yard No	1033
Built	1987
Entered service with P&O	1987
Engines	4 Sulzer Diesels
Speed (knots)	18.5
Call sign	PGJW
Usual route	Hull-Europoort

Gross tons	31,785
Net	18,197
Deadweight	6,419
Length (o.a.)	179.20m
Breadth (Extr.)	25.40m
Draught (max)	6.13m
Passenger capacity	1,250
Vehicles (max)	850 cars/ 180 Trailers
Builders	Govan Shipbuilders Ltd, Glasgow, UK
Yard No	265
Built	1987
Entered service with P&O	1987
Engines	4 Sulzer Diesels
Speed (knots)	18.5
Call sign	GIFR
Usual route	Hull-Europoort

Philippe Holthof

John Hendy

Gross tons	26,290
Net	10,568
Deadweight	5,586
Length (o.a.)	173.29m
Breadth (Extr.)	25.20m
Draught (max)	6.02m
Passenger capacity	881
Vehicles (max)	519 cars/179 Trailers
Builders	AG Weser, Seebeckwerft, Bremerhaven, Germany
Yard No	972
Built	1974
Entered service with P&O	1974
Engines	2 Stork-Werkspoor Diesels
Speed (knots)	18.5
Call sign	GUBH
Usual route	Hull-Zeebrugge

Gross tons	26,919
Net	10,413
Deadweight	5,658
Length (o.a.)	173.29m
Breadth (Extr.)	25.20m
Draught (max)	6.02m
Passenger capacity	881
Vehicles (max)	519 cars/179 Trailers
Builders	AG Weser, Seebeckwerft, Bremerhaven, Germany
Yard No	973
Built	1974
Entered service with P&O	1974
Engines	2 Stork-Werkspoor Diesels
Speed (knots)	18.5
Call sign	PGJY
Usual route	Hull-Zeebrugge

P&O North Sea Ferries

Miles Cowsill

Gross tons	17,884		**Gross tons**	17,884
Net	5,366		**Net**	5,366
Deadweight	11,400		**Deadweight**	11,400
Length (o.a.)	170.93m		**Length (o.a.)**	170.93m
Breadth (Extr.)	23.04m		**Breadth (Extr.)**	23.04m
Draught (max)	7.62m		**Draught (max)**	7.62m
Passenger capacity	12		**Passenger capacity**	12
Vehicles (max)	145 x 12m freight units		**Vehicles (max)**	145 x 12m freight units
Builders	Rauma-Repola Oy, Rauma, Finland		**Builders**	Rauma-Repola Oy, Rauma, Finland
Yard No	260		**Yard No**	261
Built	1980		**Built**	1980
Entered service with P&O	1991		**Entered service with P&O**	1991
Engines	2 MaK Diesels		**Engines**	2 MaK Diesels
Speed (knots)	19.0		**Speed (knots)**	19.0
Call sign	OIKP		**Call sign**	OIKQ
Usual route	Middlesbrough-Europoort		**Usual route**	Middlesbrough-Europoort
Former Name	*Bore King*		**Former Name**	*Bore Queen*

Philippe Holthof

P&O North Sea Ferries

Gross tons	17,464
Net	5,239
Deadweight	6,791
Length (o.a.)	166.77m
Breadth (Extr.)	23.90m
Draught (max)	6.02m
Passenger capacity	114
Vehicles (max)	156 x 12m freight units
Builders	Van der Giessen de Noord B.V., Krimpen aan den IJssel, Netherlands
Yard No	961
Built	1993
Entered service with P&O	1993
Engines	4 Sulzer Diesels
Speed (knots)	23.0
Call sign	PGIS
Usual route	Hull-Europoort

Gross tons	17,464
Net	5,239
Deadweight	6,722
Length (o.a.)	166.77m
Breadth (Extr.)	23.90m
Draught (max)	6.02m
Passenger capacity	114
Vehicles (max)	156 x 12m freight units
Builders	Van der Giessen de Noord B.V., Krimpen aan den IJssel, Netherlands
Yard No	962
Built	1994
Entered service with P&O	1994
Engines	4 Sulzer Diesels
Speed (knots)	23.0
Call sign	MSLN2
Usual route	Hull-Europoort

John Hendy

John Hendy

Gross tons	14,087
Net	4,226
Deadweight	5,024
Length (o.a.)	150.02m
Breadth (Extr.)	20.73m
Draught (max)	5.12m
Passenger capacity	12
Vehicles (max)	125 x 12m freight units
Builders	Mitsui Engineering & SB Co Ltd, Tamano, Japan
Yard No	1164
Built	1979
Entered service with P&O	1989
Engines	2 Mitsui Diesels
Speed (knots)	19.4
Call sign	PGJL
Usual route	Hull-Zeebrugge
Former Names	*Tipperary, Puma*

Gross tons	19,992
Net	5,998
Deadweight	11,500
Length (o.a.)	180.00m
Breadth (Extr.)	25.20m
Draught (max)	6.00m
Passenger capacity	12
Vehicles (max)	210 x 12m freight units
Builders	Aker Finnyards, Rauma, Finland
Yard No	424
Built	1999
Entered service with P&O	1999
Engines	2 Wartsila Diesels
Speed (knots)	21.0
Call sign	PCCC
Usual route	Middlesbrough-Zeebrugge

Miles Cowsill

FotoFlite

Gross tons	19,992
Net	5,998
Deadweight	11,500
Length (o.a.)	180.00m
Breadth (Extr.)	25.20m
Draught (max)	6.00m
Passenger capacity	12
Vehicles (max)	210 x 12m freight units
Builders	Aker Finnyards, Rauma, Finland
Yard No	425
Built	1999
Entered service with P&O	1999
Engines	2 Wartsila Diesels
Speed (knots)	21.0
Call sign	PCCD
Usual route	Middlesbrough-Zeebrugge

Gross tons	21,162
Net	6,348
Deadweight	8,734
Length (o.a.)	184.61m
Breadth (Extr.)	25.28m
Draught (max)	6.37m
Passenger capacity	166
Vehicles (max)	150 x 12m freight units
Builders	Hyundai HI, Ulsan, South Korea
Yard No	649
Built	1978
Entered service with P&O	1986.
Engines	2 Pielstick Diesels
Speed (knots)	17.0
Call sign	GFWR
Usual route	Felixstowe-Europoort
Former Names	*Cerdic Ferry, StenaTransporter, Syria, Alpha Enterprise*

FotoFlite

Miles Cowsill

Gross tons	21,162
Net	6,348
Deadweight	8,672
Length (o.a.)	184.61m
Breadth (Extr.)	25.28m
Draught (max)	6.37m
Passenger capacity	166
Vehicles (max)	150 x 12m freight units
Builders	Hyundai HI, Ulsan, South Korea
Yard No	643
Built	1977
Entered service with P&O	1986
Engines	2 Pielstick Diesels
Speed (knots)	17.0
Call sign	GFVM
Usual route	Felixstowe-Europoort
Former Names	*Doric Ferry, Hellas, Alpha Progress, Stena Runner*

Gross tons	16,776
Net	5,032
Deadweight	5,465
Length (o.a.)	151.01m
Breadth (Extr.)	23.58m
Draught (max)	6.50m
Passenger capacity	124
Vehicles (max)	110 x 12m freight units
Builders	Hyundai HI, Ulsan, South Korea
Yard No	651
Built	1978
Entered service with P&O	1981
Engines	2 Pielstick Diesels
Speed (knots)	17.0
Call sign	GZOL
Usual route	Felixstowe-Europoort
Former Names	*Nordic Ferry, Merzario Hispania, Merzario Espania*

Roger Hurford

Roger Hurford

Gross tons	16,776
Net	5,032
Deadweight	5,336
Length (o.a.)	151.01m
Breadth (Extr.)	23.58m
Draught (max)	6.50m
Passenger capacity	124
Vehicles (max)	110 x 12m freight units
Builders	Hyundai HI, Ulsan, South Korea
Yard No	652
Built	1978
Entered service with P&O	1981
Engines	2 Pielstick Diesels
Speed (knots)	17.0
Call sign	GZOM
Usual route	Felixstowe-Europoort
Former Names	*Baltic Ferry, Finnrose, Stena Transporter*

Gross tons	6,568
Net	1,970
Deadweight	4,465
Length (o.a.)	135.05m
Breadth (Extr.)	16.51m
Draught (max)	4.74m
Passenger capacity	6
Vehicles (max)	75 trailers
Builders	Kariskronavarvet AB, Kariskrona, Sweden
Yard No	397
Built	1980
Entered service with P&O	1999*
Engines	2 Polar Diesels
Speed (knots)	16.0
Call sign	SHWB
Usual route	Felixstowe-Zeebrugge
Former Name	*Balder Dona*

Miles Cowsill

P&O North Sea Ferries

Gross tons	6,568
Net	1,970
Deadweight	4,465
Length (o.a.)	135.35m
Breadth (Extr.)	16.51m
Draught (max)	4.74m
Passenger capacity	6
Vehicles (max)	75 trailers
Builders	Kariskronavarvet AB, Kariskrona, Sweden
Yard No	398
Built	1980
Entered service with P&O	1999*
Engines	2 Polar Diesels
Speed (knots)	16.0
Call sign	SHWA
Usual route	Felixstowe-Zeebrugge
Former Names	*Azua, Rovinga, Balder Vinga*

Gross tons	60,600
Net	-
Deadweight	8,850
Length (o.a.)	215.00m
Breadth (Extr.)	31.50m
Draught (max)	6.30m
Passenger capacity	1,360
Vehicles (max)	250 cars + 400 freight units
Builders	Fincantieri, Venice, Italy
Yard No	6065/6066
Built	2001
Entered service with P&O	2001
Engines	4 Wartsila Diesels
Speed (knots)	22.0
Call signs	-
Route operation	Hull-Europoort

CHAPTER 10

P&O Scottish Ferries

The passages across some of the roughest stretches of water surrounding our coasts can be exceptionally rough and even today there remain periods of inclement weather during which time the vessels are unable to sail. It is, however, the proud boast of the company that during its long existence not one person has been lost in any accident involving one of its ships.

Historically the company traded under the illustrious name of the North of Scotland, Orkney & Shetland Shipping Co. Ltd. which was always conveniently abbreviated to the 'North Co.' The old North Co, was an amalgamation of a number of small and competing concerns which joined forces in June 1875 offering services from Aberdeen and Leith. The routes offered by the company provided a lifeline to the islands importing coal, timber and other commodities while the export of livestock has always been confined to a short annual period.

The port of Scrabster (two miles from Thurso) was opened during the 1850s and on its arrival in the Caithness town in 1874, the Highland Railway Company sought to operate its own steamer across the Pentland Firth to Stromness. This was accomplished three years later but in 1882 the North Co. steamer *St. Olaf* took over its working. Ten years later the first *St. Ola* took up the link and since that time, this famous name has always been associated with the Pentland Firth crossing.

St.Ola. (John May)

The services and ships provided a century ago certainly appear very generous when compared with those of today. Three sailings each week were provided from Leith to Orkney and Shetland and all called at Aberdeen en route. The first, known as the west-side boat, sailed via Stromness (Orkney) and Scalloway (Shetland). The second, the 'secondary indirect boat,' was via Kirkwall (Orkney) and Lerwick (Shetland) whilst the third (the 'weekend boat') followed the same route with the additional call at the Caithness port of Wick. An additional sailing to Wick and Thurso was called the 'Caithness boat.' Direct sailings linking Aberdeen with Lerwick were instituted in 1891 with the company providing the new *St. Giles* in the following year. Meanwhile, expansion in tourist traffic saw popular cruises to Norway in the *St. Sunniva* and the construction of the company's own hotel at Hillswick (Shetland) in 1902.

During the period immediately prior to the First World War, the North Co. provided the islands with the best service they have ever experienced. Shetland was served five times a week from Leith and Aberdeen, Orkney was served three times while Caithness received two sailings.

During the 1914-18 War the North Co. lost three ships, the *St. Nicholas, St. Magnus* and the *St. Margaret* and in order to bide things over, cargo ships were acquired for the first time - the first to be built for the company being the *St. Clement* in 1928.

Competition from the airways first occurred during the mid-1930s and a daily air mail link to Shetland was commenced in 1938. The outbreak of World War Two was also to see the North Co. in the thick of it. More losses were recorded in the form of the second *St. Sunniva, St. Catherine, St. Clement* and the *St. Fergus*. Towards the war's end, only two vessels, the *St. Magnus* (Aberdeen - Lerwick) and *St. Rognvald* (Aberdeen - Kirkwall) were available for passenger service while Leith was served by cargo vessels. Fortunately the *St. Clair* and the *Earl of Zetland* both returned safely from hostilities as did the *St. Ninian* which in view of her age was not returned to service.

The post-war pattern of services was greatly reduced with the Caithness link being made by cargo boat only until its demise in 1956. Gradually calls to centres in Orkney and Shetland other than to Kirkwall, Stromness and Lerwick (many serviced by 'flitboats' tendering to the steamers which had anchored offshore) were withdrawn leaving smaller operators and then the respective councils to provide for the transhipment of passengers and cargoes.

In 1961 the company was taken over by Coast Lines Ltd which, ten years later, was duly absorbed into the P&O Group which was then seeking to expand its interests into the lucrative Irish Sea road haulage and freight markets. The title P&O Ferries (Orkney & Shetland Services) was adopted in October 1975 becoming P&O Scottish Ferries in 1989.

Roll on - roll off services came to the Pentland Firth link when in January 1975 the third *St. Ola* entered service. She was followed by the *Rof Beaver* (ie Roll on ferry *Beaver*) which entered service from Leith in May 1975 while Southampton's *SF Panther* (withdrawn from her San Sebastian sailings in November 1975) was converted for the new Aberdeen - Lerwick ro-ro service and renamed *St. Clair*. After many delays the new service eventually opened in April 1977.

*The **St. Rognvald** currently maintains the Aberdeen-Lerwick freight service for P&O Scottish Ferries. She is seen here at Lerwick.* (Miles Cowsill)

Today's fleet consists of the new *St. Clair*, which entered service in March 1992 after seeing service in the Western Channel with Brittany Ferries, the *St. Ola* on the Pentland Firth link which after a career operating in the Baltic also took up service with P&O in March 1992 and the third vessel *St. Sunniva* which was built for an internal Danish service and latterly ran for P&O Normandy Ferries between Dover and Boulogne. She was told to P&O Scottish Ferries in 1987 and since then has provided a regular service from Aberdeen - Stromness - Lerwick. Freight services are currently operated by the *St. Rognvald* and, although the ships are all reliable units to operate, plans for replacements very much depend on whether or not P&O are given the franchise to continue operating the North services into the new millennium.

*Captured in the morning sun, the **St. Ola** is seen here pending her departure from Stromness to Scrabster. (P&O Scottish Ferries)*

ST CLAIR

Colin Smith

Gross tons	8,696
Net	3,517
Deadweight	1,021
Length (o.a.)	118.01m
Breadth (Extr.)	19.60m·
Draught (max)	5.03m
Passenger capacity	406
Vehicles (max)	370 cars/38 Lorries
Builders	Schiffbau-Ges. Unterweser AG, Bremerhaven, Germany
Yard No	478
Built	1971
Entered service with P&O	1991
Engines	2 MAN Diesels
Speed (knots)	18.0
Call sign	MPRL6
Usual route	Aberdeen-Lerwick
Former Names	*Treg, Tregastel, Njegos, Travemunde*

ST SUNNIVA

P&O

Gross tons	6,350
Net	2,151
Deadweight	1,045
Length (o.a.)	104.04m
Breadth (Extr.)	18.93m
Draught (max)	4.61m
Passenger capacity	400
Vehicles (max)	230 cars/28 Lorries
Builders	Helsingor S&M, Helsingor, Denmark
Yard No	399
Built	1972
Entered service with P&O	1979
Engines	2 Stork-Werkspoor Diesels
Speed (knots)	16.0
Call sign	GBCG
Usual route	Aberdeen-Stromness-Lerwick
Former Names	*nf Panther, Lasse II, Djursland*

ST ROGNVALD

ST OLA

Colin Smith

John May

	ST ROGNVALD		ST OLA
Gross tons	5,297	Gross tons	4,833
Net	1,589	Net	1,449
Deadweight	3,810	Deadweight	711
Length (o.a.)	103.76m	Length (o.a.)	85.95m
Breadth (Extr.)	18.78m	Breadth (Extr.)	16.77m
Draught (max)	5.03m	Draught (max)	4.00m
Passenger capacity	12	Passenger capacity	600
Vehicles (max)	47 Lorries	Vehicles (max)	180 cars/14 Lorries
Builders	Orenstein & Koppel AG, Lubeck, Germany	Builders	Meyer, Papenburg, Germany
Yard No	671	Yard No	564
Built	1970	Built	1971
Entered service with P&O	1989	Entered service with P&O	1991
Engines	2 MaK Diesels	Engines	4 Wartsila Diesels
Speed (knots)	16.0	Speed (knots)	17.0
Call sign	GJWT	Call sign	MPLG3
Usual route	Aberdeen-Lerwick	Usual route	Scrabster-Stromness
Former Names	*Marino Torre, Rhone, Rhonetal*	Former Names	*Eck, Eckero, Svea Scarlett*

CHAPTER 11

P&O Nedlloyd

The origin of the P&O element of today's fleet of 120 owned, leased and chartered ships goes back to 1965 and the formation by P&O, British and Commonwealth, Furness Withy and Ocean Steamship of Overseas Containers Limited, to investigate and eventually containerise the cargo liner routes of all four participants. When purpose-built container ships began to be introduced in 1969, each partner owned its own ships, which were built for its own services. The initial contribution from P&O at the start of containerisation of the Australian service was the 27,000 gross ton sisters *Moreton Bay* and *Discovery Bay*. The next P&O ship to join OCL was the 35,000 gross ton *Osaka Bay*, which entered the fleet in 1972 at the start of upgrading the Far East routes.

P&O Nedlloyd Southampton. (FotoFlite)

Although each company began with a 25% stake in OCL, these shares were adjusted in accordance with the trades being absorbed from member companies. As the replacement of general cargo liners by container ships took greater effect, P&O General Cargo Division took over responsibility for P&O's share of OCL in 1973. Over the next eight or so years the remainder of the general cargo fleet were replaced by containerships, as the last of the routes converted to cellular operation. Following the withdrawal of Furness Withy after its purchase by C Y Tung, the remaining partners exercised their options to buy its OCL shares, giving P&O almost a 50% share in the consortium by 1980.

During the early 1980's ownership of the P&O container ships was transferred to OCL, but these vessels found their way back into the P&O fleet in 1986 when the Company bought out the remaining shares held by British & Commonwealth and Ocean Transport and Trading. This gave P&O a fleet of 22 container ships and, quite cleverly, the operation became P&OCL (P&O Containers Limited).

The 1990's were a period of co-operation, acquisition and rationalisation within the container industry. In 1991 a new joint service was established with Maersk Line on the Far East run, and in the following year Cunard Ellerman's Australian container interests were acquired and absorbed into the company. By the end of 1993 P&OCL was the world's sixth largest operator in terms of capacity, carrying almost one million TEU's (twenty foot equivalent units). P&OCL, as a conference operator, was beginning to feel the effects of rate cutting by independent operators, and to balance falling revenues, economies had to be made. The logical route was by acquisition or merger, and this time the latter course was chosen. In September 1996 the merger was announced between P&OCL and the Dutch Nedlloyd Line, part of the Royal Nedlloyd Group, to form

*P&O Nedlloyd container service operates throughout the world. These two views show the **P&O Nedlloyd Southampton** on passage in the English Channel.* (FotoFlite)

a new joint venture company, P&O Nedlloyd Container Line. This amalgamation, incorporated in the UK and owned 50:50 by the participants, came into being late on 31st December 1996 in the UK (early on 1st January 1997 in the Netherlands), and was then ranked third largest in the world. By the end of 1997 cost savings of more than $200 million per annum had been achieved.

In a further consolidating move, Blue Star Line (specialising in the north/south refrigerated cargo trades) was acquired in April 1998. Later that year P&O Nedlloyd took delivery of its largest ships to date, the four 81,000 gross ton 6,700 TEU class whose lead-ship was the *P&O Nedlloyd Southampton*.

As a result of the British Government's promise to introduce a tonnage based corporation tax regime for ship-owners, P&O Chairman, Lord Sterling, pledged to re-flag at least 50 ships to the Red Ensign. The first such re-flagging took place with much publicity in September 1999, when the *Peninsular Bay* left the Bahamian registry for that of the UK.

Although P&O Nedlloyd is the third largest operator, and carried almost 2.8 million TEU's in 1999, it still only has an estimated 4.3% share of global capacity, so further mergers or purchases seem likely before the long term goal of a stock market floatation is realised. Small acquisitions such as Harrison Line's East African service and Tasman Express Line have taken place, but at the time of writing no major deal has been struck.

CHAPTER 12

Associated Bulk Carriers

P&O's entry into the dry bulk cargo market occurred in 1965, when the first bulk carrier, the *Atherstone*, with a deadweight (cargo capacity) tonnage of 40,000, was delivered. The name Associated Bulk Carriers first arose at this time as this was the name given to the joint venture company set up with Anglo Norness to operate this type of ship. The P&O subsidiary Hain-Nourse, a merger of the long established tramp operator Hains and the former liner companies James Nourse and Asiatic Steam Navigation, were the managers of the group bulk carrier fleet at that time.

The P&O Bulk Shipping Division took control of both the tanker and bulk carrier fleets on its formation in 1971. No long-term future was seen for the large oil tankers, and as their charters ended they were sold, so by 1992 this type of ship had disappeared from the fleet.

The bulk carrier fleet grew further in 1973 with the acquisition by P&O of a half share in its ABC partner, by now called Zapata Norness, but renamed Anglo Nordic. This company also operated tankers and chemical carriers. However, by the late 1970's, the bulk trades had begun to decline and most of the bulk carrier fleet was sold. Anglo Nordic was wound up, P&O took full control of ABC in 1983 and the company was renamed P&O Bulk Carriers. Several second-hand ships entered the bulk carrier fleet as trades began to improve, but no new ships were delivered until 1986, when the Japanese built *Ormond* arrived.

On the demise of the General Cargo Division, P&O Bulk Carriers was re-styled P&O Bulk Shipping, and the mainstream fleet in 1989 consisted of six bulk carriers, with a further two on order, and three tankers. Anything up to ten bulk carriers might be on short-term charter at any one time.

Over the next eight years P&O Bulk Carriers continued to moderise its fleet of Capesize (too large for the Suez Canal) ships in sometimes difficult trading conditions, but in 1997 the Company announced the formation of a new joint venture with the Chinese industrial group, Shougang. Reviving the old name Associated Bulk

*Associated Bulk Carriers' **Buccleuch** passing through the Dover Strait.* (FotoFite)

Carriers, this 50:50 partnership controlled one of the world's largest independent fleet of Capesize bulk carriers.

Following a particularly difficult trading period and as charter rates began to improve, P&O acquired the remaining 50% of ABC from Shougang on 3rd April 2000 for a nominal sum. P&O also announced its intention to float ABC on the Oslo Stock Exchange at the earliest opportunity.

*The **Duhallow** is seen in the English Channel.* (FotoFlite)

Container Ships
(All operated by P&O Nedlloyd Container Line in which P&O has a 50% interest)

	Gross Tons
America Star	24,907
Arafura	37,902
Aramac	52,007
Argentina Star	22,635
Ariake	37,286
Berlin Express	41,814
City of Cape Town	52,055
Colombo Bay	50,350
Heemskerck	51,982
Jervis Bay	50,235
Mairangi Bay	43,674
Marin	11,217
Melbourne Star	24,907
Mercosul Argentina	19,636
Nedlloyd Africa	48,508
Nedlloyd America	48,508
Nedlloyd Asia	48,508
Nedlloyd Clarence	33,405
Nedlloyd Clement	33,405
Nedlloyd Colombo	32,114
Nedlloyd Europa	48,508
Nedlloyd Hongkong	56,248
Nedlloyd Honshu	56,248
Nedlloyd Hoorn	52,007
Nedlloyd Oceania	48,508
New Zealand Pacific	43,704
Newport Bay	50,235
Oriental Bay*	50,538
P&O Nedlloyd Auckland*	31,333
P&O Nedlloyd Brisbane	37,814
P&O Nedlloyd Beunos Aires	23,790

P&O Nedlloyd Rotterdam. (P&O)

P&O Nedlloyd Genoa *	31,333
P&O Nedlloyd Houston	23,790
P&O Nedlloyd Jakarta*	31,333
P&O Nedlloyd Kobe	80,942
P&O Nedlloyd Kowloon	80,942
P&O Nedlloyd Los Angeles	30,175
P&O Nedlloyd Lyttleton	27,910
P&O Nedlloyd Marseille*	31,333
P&O Nedlloyd Mercator	66,526
P&O Nedlloyd Napier	25,407
P&O Nedlloyd Piraeus	31,207
P&O Nedlloyd Rotterdam*	80,942
P&O Nedlloyd Southampton	80,942
P&O Nedlloyd Sydney*	31,333
P&O Nedlloys Taranaki	29,259
P&O Nedlloyd Tasman	66,526
P&O Nedlloyd Tauranga	25,093
P&O Nedlloyd Vera Cruz	23,790
Palliser Bay	44,150
Pegasus Bay	52,055
Peninsular Bay	50,538
Providence Bay	50,350

Queensland Star	25,031
Repulse Bay	50,235
Resolution Bay	43,674
Shenzhen Bay	50,350
Singapore Bay	50,235
Sydney Star	24,907
Texas	56,822

Bulk carriers
(All operated by Associated Bulk Carriers, a wholly owned subsidiary)

	Gross Tons
Aberous*	77,273
Buccleuch*	90,820
Cotswold	80,578
Duhallow	63,240
Eridge	63,153
Fernie*	63,153
Grafton*	63,153
Heythrop	85,364
Irfon*	84,921
Kildare	108,083
Meynell	93,629
Newforest	93,629
Ormond	96,659
Pytchley	92,194
Quorn	92,194
Rutland	85,848
Snowdon	85,848
Taunton	95,835
Ullswater	63,106
Vine	63,106
Waterford	77,096
York	77,113
Zetland	74,003

Other Cargo Vessels

	Gross Tons
Aburri	2,700
Kamora	2,029
Kopi	1,317
Western Endeavour	2,754
Western Enterprise	2,754
Western Flyer	2,146
Western Star	2,146
Western Triumph	2,143
Western Zenith	2,143

Research, Supply and other Service Vessels

	Gross Tons
Aurora Australis	6,574
Far Minara	1,631
Far Sea	2,285
Golden Glory	292
Lady Audrey	1,978
Lady Caroline	1,179
Lady Cynthia	1,997
Lady Dawn	1,267
Lady Elaine	2,127
Lady Elizabeth	1,924
Lady Kari-Ann	1,924
Lady Sandra	2,599
Lady Valisia	1,972
Seahorse Mercator	212
Seahorse Spirit	2,090
Seahorse Standard	2,090
Shelf Ranger	1,597
Western Hope	229
Western Venturer	185

Other Ferries in P&O Fleet

	Gross Tons
Elk	14,374
P&OSL Picardy+	13,601
Reef Adventurer II	192
Stena Invicta+	19,763

New Cruise Vessels on Order

		Gross Tons
P&O Cruises		
Fincantieri No 6067	2004	108,806
Aida Cruises		
Aker MTW No 003	2002	42,200
Aker MTW No 004	2003	42,200
Princess Cruises		
Golden Princess	2001	108,806
Fincantieri No 6051	2001	108,806
Chantiers de l'Atlantique		
No C32	2002	88,000
No D32	2003	88,000
Mitsubishi No 2180	2003	113,000
Mitsubishi No 2181	2004	113,000

Other Vessels on Order

		Gross Tons
P&O Nedlloyd Barentsz	2000	64,000
P&O Nedlloyd Drake	2000	64,000
P&O Nedlloyd Hudson	2000	64,000
Hyundai No 1274	2000	88,700
Hyundai No 1275	2000	88,700
Hyundai No 1276	2000	88,700
Hyundai No 1277	2000	88,700

Key to Fleet Information
* On charter
+ For Sale

Acknowledgements

The authors are grateful to the following for assistance with this title:
Stephen Rabson (P&O Group), Brenda Mayes, Richard Mayes, Gillian Ridgway, Penny Guy (P&O Portsmouth), Chris Laming (P&O Stena Line), Jim Pybus (P&O North Sea Ferries), James Essler (P&O Irish Sea), Gordon Hislip, Roger Hurford, Andrew Lowe (Haven Colourprint), Pat Somner and Angie Truman (Ferry Publications)